The Massey Lectures Series

The Massey Lectures are co-sponsored by CBC Radio, House of Anansi Press, and Massey College in the University of Toronto. The series was created in honour of the Right Honourable Vincent Massey, former governor general of Canada, and was inaugurated in 1961 to enable distinguished authorities to communicate the results of original study on subjects of contemporary interest.

This book comprises the 2004 Massey Lectures, "A Short History of Progress," broadcast in November 2004 as part of CBC Radio's *Ideas* series. The producer of the series was Philip Coulter; the executive producer was Bernie Lucht.

Ronald Wright

Novelist, historian, and essayist Ronald Wright is the author of ten books of fiction and nonfiction; he has been published in eighteen languages and more than forty countries. His CBC Massey Lectures, *A Short History of Progress*, won the Libris Award for Nonfiction Book of the Year and inspired Martin Scorsese's 2011 documentary film *Surviving Progress*. His other bestsellers include *Time Among the Maya*, *What Is America?*, and *Stolen Continents*, an award-winning history of the Americas since 1492. Wright's first novel, the dystopia *A Scientific Romance*, won Britain's David Higham Prize and was chosen as a book of the year by the *New York Times*, the *Globe and Mail*, and the *Sunday Times*. His latest work, *The Gold Eaters*, is a novel set during the conquest of Peru. Born in England to Canadian and British parents, Wright studied archaeology and anthropology at Cambridge and the University of Calgary. He lives on Canada's West Coast. ronaldwright.com.

ALSO BY RONALD WRIGHT

FICTION

Henderson's Spear

A Scientific Romance

The Gold Eaters

HISTORY

*What Is America?: A Short History of the New
World Order*

*Stolen Continents: Conquest and Resistance in
the Americas*

TRAVEL AND ARCHAEOLOGY

Time Among the Maya

On Fiji Islands

Cut Stones and Crossroads: A Journey in Peru

ESSAYS

Home and Away

A SHORT HISTORY
OF PROGRESS

by RONALD WRIGHT

ANANSI

First published in Canada in 2004 by House of Anansi Press Inc.
This edition published in Canada in 2019 and the USA in 2021 by House of Anansi Press Inc.
www.houseofanansi.com

CBC and Massey College logos used with permission.

Permission is gratefully acknowledged to reprint excerpts from the following:

(pp. 65–66, 70, 75–76, 77) *The Epic of Gilgamesh*, translated by N. K. Sandars (Penguin Classics 1960, Third edition 1972). Copyright © N. K. Sandars, 1960, 1964, 1972.
Used by permission of Penguin Group UK.

(pp. vii, 88–89) *Amores* by Ovid, translated by Guy Lee (John Murray, 1968), republished in
2000 as *Ovid in Love*. Copyright © 1968 Guy Lee. Used by courtesy of John Murray.

Every reasonable effort has been made to contact the holders of copyright for materials
quoted in this work. The publishers will gladly receive information that will enable them
to rectify any inadvertent errors or omissions in subsequent editions.

House of Anansi Press is committed to protecting our natural environment.
This book is made of material from well-managed FSC®-certified forests, recycled
materials, and other controlled sources.

25 24 23 22 21   2 3 4 5 6

Library and Archives Canada Cataloguing in Publication

Title: A short history of progress / Ronald Wright.
Names: Wright, Ronald, author.
Series: Massey lectures series.
Description: Fifteenth anniversary edition. | Series statement: The CBC Massey lectures
Identifiers: Canadiana 20190064641 | ISBN 9781487006983 (softcover)
Subjects: LCSH: Progress—History. | LCSH: Civilization—History. | LCSH:
Environmental degradation.
Classification: LCC CB69 .W75 2019 | DDC 909—dc23

Cover design: Bill Douglas
Cover photograph: The Image Bank / Michael Kelley
Typesetting: Brian Panhuyzen

Canada Council   Conseil des Arts   ONTARIO ARTS COUNCIL
for the Arts   du Canada   CONSEIL DES ARTS DE L'ONTARIO

*We acknowledge for their financial support of our publishing program the Canada Council
for the Arts, the Ontario Arts Council, and the Government of Canada.*

Printed and bound in Canada

MIX
Paper from
responsible sources
FSC® C103567

For my mother,
Shirley Phyllis Wright

Long ago . . .
No one tore the ground with ploughshares
or parcelled out the land
or swept the sea with dipping oars —
the shore was the world's end.
Clever human nature, victim of your inventions,
disastrously creative,
why cordon cities with towered walls?
Why arm for war?

— Ovid, *Amores,* Book 3

Acknowledgments

My thanks to Bernie Lucht and John Fraser for their support. To Martha Sharpe at Anansi and Philip Coulter at the CBC for their skilful editing and helpful suggestions. To Richard Outram, Farley Mowat, Brian Brett, Jonathan Bennett, and Janice Boddy for their kindness in reading the manuscript and for many valuable comments. To Sarah MacLachlan at Anansi for suggesting this fifteenth-anniversary edition; to Janie Yoon and Maria Golikova at Anansi for their editorial expertise. And to my wife, Deborah Campbell, for her encouragement and help.

Contents

INTRODUCTION TO THE ANNIVERSARY EDITION

THIS BOOK WAS inspired by ancient people who built a great city in the Guatemalan jungle, then abandoned it more than a thousand years ago. I'd been to the ruins of Tikal many times, and each time I saw things I hadn't seen or understood before. The Maya city is so big and thickly overgrown it takes days to climb the temples rearing like skyscrapers from the jungle canopy, to wander through silent courtyards and dark rooms of labyrinthine palaces. And that is only the downtown core, marked by its cluster of limestone towers. The suburbs, covering fifty square miles,[1] are still cloaked in jungle, now a wildlife sanctuary echoing each dawn and dusk with the throaty roars of howler monkeys. One evening in the twilight I glimpsed a jaguar, a dark shape flowing through the bush, who seemed to follow me for a tense half hour along an ancient causeway. It was Tikal's very scale — like that of a modern city — which nudged my thoughts from past to future. What will our own great cities look like centuries from now? Will they be beautiful ruins? What brings such places down?

Spurred by a gathering unease about our ecological crisis, these thoughts led to my first novel, a dystopian satire in which London ends up rather like Tikal.[2] When I was asked a few years later to give the CBC Massey Lectures, I decided to write more explicitly about the catastrophic fall of past civilizations and what we might learn from them to avoid a similar fate. The underlying pattern to the cases I examined was that all became victims of their own success. None was able to reform or adapt effectively, and most didn't even try — at least, not until it was too late. This gave me the idea of the *progress trap*: a seductive chain of successes that, upon reaching a certain scale, leads to disaster.

Since this book first came out, it has gone into nearly twenty languages and reached some half million readers around the world; it also inspired Martin Scorsese's 2011 film *Surviving Progress*. For this fifteenth-anniversary edition, I asked myself what many people have been asking me: Am I more or less hopeful than I was in 2004? I considered whether parts of the book might need rewriting or rethinking. Of course, much has happened since then, some of it encouraging. Yet the main flow of events has not wavered from the alarming course we can read in both the deep past and the latest scientific reports. Rather than tinkering with the original text, I'll outline some relevant findings here, then touch on our predicament today.

FIRST, TO THE PAST: a comforting place because no one can change it; it is simply what it was, whether we understand it well or not. But even though we will never know everything that happened there, the more we can learn, the better — for the past tells us who we are. Over the last fifteen years, knowledge of our prehistory has grown as quickly as forebodings for our future. Some interpretations and dates must be reviewed in light of new findings, while others that were still moot in 2004 — our close kinship with Neanderthals, for example — have since been confirmed. Of special interest are the tales of two caves, and a revolution in human genetics that promises to be the biggest anthropological breakthrough since the discovery of radiocarbon dating in the 1950s.

Just weeks after this book came off the press in 2004, news broke that bones of an unknown and rather odd human species had been found in a cave on the island of Flores, Indonesia. Nicknamed "hobbits" for their size, *Homo floresiensis* adults were barely half the size of ourselves and other human forebears. Even more puzzling, their skulls seemed to resemble very early African fossils from 2 or 3 million years ago. Yet here they were in tropical Asia, on an island cut off by deep water, living on till a mere 50,000 years ago — quite modern times in human evolution. Suspected at first to be a hoax or a group suffering from deformities after becoming stranded and inbred, they are now accepted as an offshoot of *Homo erectus* or an unidentified forerunner, thriving in isolation from the rest of mankind for more than a million years. Unhappily, the fate that awaited these little folk seems to have fulfilled William Golding's pessimism in his novel *The Inheritors*. Their world came to a sudden end when people like ourselves, spreading across Asia, reached Flores and killed them off.[3]

As if one game-changing discovery were not enough, in 2008 archaeologists dug a young girl's finger bone from a roomy cave in southern Siberia that had already yielded many animal and human remains, including those of a Neanderthal from 120,000 years ago and "modern" (Cro-Magnon) people. Unlike the Flores cave, this one was cold enough to preserve ancient DNA. Genetic analysis has revealed that the finger's owner, who died about 50,000 years ago, belonged to a third human subspecies, hitherto unknown. Since the cave was called Denisova — after a hermit named Denis who lived there in the eighteenth century — the girl's mystery folk are called Denisovans.

Evidently, three kinds of people had lived in Denis's cave at one time or another. Then, in 2018, another extraordinary find showed that two of them had done so simultaneously: DNA from an adolescent girl who died some 90,000 years ago proved that her mother was Neanderthal and her father Denisovan, the only first-generation example of interbreeding between human subspecies ever found.[4] This was truly a jackpot, especially since Denisovan bones are vanishingly rare: just a handful of fragments and teeth all told. Never before has so much (as Churchill might have said) been learned from so little about so few.

Or so many; for over the last ten years, a revolution in genome analysis has thrown open the book of human roamings and couplings from a million years ago until the present.[5] While much is still to be filled in, especially from Asia and tropical regions, comparisons of ancient and modern DNA samples have traced out the human story with a new degree of likelihood and detail. The surprises are many. For one, "archaic" features on modern skulls (not least my own[6]) do indeed reflect mingling between Neanderthals and the forebears of all today's humans north of the Sahara.[7] While Denisovan ancestry is absent from most Europeans, Africans, and Asians, it is found in peoples of New Guinea, Australia, and the Pacific islands — all a very long way from Denis's man-cave.[8]

Clearly, a "family tree" metaphor is no longer very helpful in picturing the human race over the last million years, for trees only branch, not blend. Our story is more like a river meandering across a silty plain, fanning out in channels, cut off in pools, remixing in floods, splitting and blending time and again. To greatly simplify complex data, it seems that three main human lines flowed down through time from shared ancestors living between roughly a third and two-thirds of a million years ago. All three hailed ultimately from Africa, and they never diverged enough to become discrete species incapable of interbreeding (unlike the Flores folk, who had split off further back).[9] Two latterly evolved in Europe and Asia, becoming the Neanderthal and Denisovan varieties; the third continued evolving in Africa, becoming the Cro-Magnons (also rather confusingly called "modern" humans). Then, between 120,000 and 50,000 years ago, the Cro-Magnons began making sorties from Africa into the Middle East. After being driven back several times, they won a solid footing in Eurasia and managed to spread throughout the landmass, displacing and mix-

ing with their long-lost cousins. By around 40,000 years
ago, the Neanderthals and Denisovans had been overrun,
though their blood still flows in most of us alive today.[10]

Moving on to relatively recent times, several discoveries have added to our understanding of ancient
civilization. The most surprising is in southern Turkey.
On the time-worn Anatolian plateau stands a mound
called Göbekli Tepe, or Potbelly Hill, covering about
twenty-two acres.[11] There, the German archaeologist
Klaus Schmidt unearthed a series of round buildings
made of T-shaped limestone pillars weighing ten tons or
more, their well-trimmed sides adorned with carvings of
animals and birds. The monuments looked much like the
work of an early civilization. But there was no trace of
any houses, let alone a town. And the dating obtained (by
both radiocarbon and stratigraphy) put the finest stonework at 11,000 years ago, soon after the end of the last
ice age, when all people in the world were still hunters
and gatherers. The Neolithic Revolution — which later
brought farming, herding, and eventually full civilization
with cities and high populations — would not bear fruit
for thousands of years.[12] Göbekli Tepe's monuments were
twice as old as they should be.

Schmidt suggested these buildings were the world's
first temples, a "ceremonial centre" where nomadic pilgrims gathered at certain times of the year and set to work
quarrying and carving. The ecology of the region was
unusually rich in those days, a true land of plenty before
a drying climate and human misuse began to degrade it.
The monuments of Göbekli Tepe speak of enough wild

resources to support specialists over generations: stone-
workers, artists, and perhaps a priesthood.

Potbelly Hill is therefore an exception to the "no civilization without cultivation" rule. But it isn't wholly alone.
Sophisticated art did arise in other hunter-gatherer societies when food supply and population rose higher than
the norm. One example is the superb cave painting of late
Palaeolithic Europe, at Lascaux, Altamira, and elsewhere.
Another is the great art and cedar architecture of the
Northwest coast of North America, where a high level
of social complexity was supported by vast salmon runs
and other natural wealth.

Göbekli Tepe's uniqueness — and precariousness —
can be seen in its decline. From time to time, for reasons
unknown, old temples were filled in and new ones raised
on top. While the building layout stayed much the same,
the later phases were roughly and hastily done, suggesting the natural bounty of Anatolia had started to run low.
The art of fine stonework was not handed down to the
future. Nothing comparable would be built anywhere on
Earth for another 5,000 years.

Leaving Göbekli Tepe aside as a remarkable anomaly,
we must next revise the long-standing belief that the
Sumerians of what is now Iraq built the world's first true
civilization: the first large towns and organized farming
based on irrigation works. Recent digs at Huaricanga
and other sites on the dry South American coast have
shown that planned towns and irrigation systems also
arose there, independently, at the same time — during
the fourth millennium B.C. A person orbiting the Earth

5,000 years ago (a few centuries before Stonehenge or the Egyptian pyramids) would have seen cities going up in two places on opposite sides of the world: Mesopotamia and Peru.[13]

A big technical advance in recent years has been the use of lidar, a kind of laser scanning, to read ancient landscapes in what are now rainforests, where remains may lie hidden beneath a thick pelt of trees. This has been done around Tikal in Guatemala, Angkor in Cambodia, and elsewhere. The effect is like time travel: centuries of vegetation are magically peeled away, revealing the lines and blocky shapes of ancient buildings, waterworks, and roads, almost as if they were still in use.

Early archaeological work at jungle ruins had been confined to great buildings, because not only were they the most impressive but also little else could be found. It was assumed the common folk had lived scattered on small farms in woodland clearings. By the late twentieth century, it was known the temples stood at the heart of true cities supported by advanced agriculture, yet many details were still unclear. Then, in 2018, lidar results covering eight hundred square miles[14] of the Guatemalan jungle were published, revealing 60,000 unknown building works, including canals, reservoirs, raised highways, terraced fields, housing, even whole towns. A further revelation was the extent of defensive walls and forts. Clearly, the jungle had been felled even more ruthlessly than I suggested in chapter 4, and warfare was chronic, as in Europe. It is likely the ancient Maya were twice as numerous as previously thought: between 10 and 15 million on the eve of the Classic collapse, a very high number for such a fragile ecology.[15]

LIKE THOSE MAYA, we too have outgrown environmental limits. In just fifteen years since this book's first edition, our numbers have risen by 1.4 billion, to a total of nearly 7.8 billion by the end of 2019. In other words, we've added another China or forty more Canadas to the world. The growth rate has fallen slightly, but consumption of resources — from fossil fuel to water, from rare earths to good earth — has risen twice as steeply, roughly doubling the impact on nature.[16] This outrunning of population by economic growth has lifted perhaps a billion of the poorest into the badly paid outskirts of the working class, mainly in China and India. Yet those in extreme poverty and hunger still number at least a billion.[17] Meanwhile, the wealthiest billion — to which most North Americans and Europeans, and many Asians, now belong — devour an ever-growing share of natural capital. The commanding heights of this group, the billionaires' club, has more than 2,200 members with a combined known worth nearing $10 trillion;[18] this super-elite not only consumes at a rate never seen before but also deploys its wealth to influence government policy, media content, and key elections.

Such, in a few words, is the shape of the human pyramid today. The 2008 crash triggered by banking fraud was staved off by money-printing and record debt. This primed a short-run recovery, which has in turn revived illusions we can borrow from nature and the future indefinitely — illusions fed by irresponsible politicians, corporate think tanks, and Panglossian cherry-pickers such as Steven Pinker. But what about the long run? In 1923, the great economist John Maynard Keynes famously answered, "In the long run we are all dead." By that he meant, let's deal with the problems we see now and leave the unforeseeable to those who come later.[19] Fair enough in the 1920s, when there was only one human on Earth for every four today, and the future seemed to have room for endless outcomes, good or bad. Nearly a century later, Keynes's quip sounds more like dire prophecy, as short-term thinking lures us ever deeper into a world-wide progress trap that science can not only observe but foresee. Predicted consequences of global warming — blighted coral reefs, melting glaciers, spreading deserts, and extreme weather — are already upon us.

One of the sad ironies of our time is that we have become very good at studying nature just as it begins to sicken and die under our weight. "Weight" is no mere metaphor: of all land mammals and birds alive today, humans and their livestock make up 96 per cent of the biomass; wildlife has dwindled to 4 per cent.[20] This has no precedent. Not so far back in history, the proportions were the other way round. As recently as 1970, humans were only half and wildlife more than twice their present numbers. These closely linked figures are milestones along our rush towards a trashed and looted planet, stripped of diversity, wildness, and resilience; strewn with waste. Such is the measure of our success.

As the proposal to name our era the "Anthropocene"

implies, humankind will leave a telltale layer in the fossil record composed of everything we produce, from mounds of chicken bones, wet-wipes, tires, mattresses, and other household waste, to metals, concrete, plastics, industrial chemicals, and the nuclear residue of power plants and weaponry. The archaeologists who dig *us* up will need to wear hazmat suits. We are cheating our children, handing them tawdry luxuries and addictive gadgets while we take away what's left of the wealth, wonder, and possibility of the pristine Earth. Calculations of humanity's footprint suggest we have been in "ecological deficit," taking more than Earth's biological systems can withstand, for at least thirty years. Topsoil is being lost between ten and forty times faster than nature can replenish it; 30 per cent of arable land has been exhausted since the mid-twentieth century.[21]

We have financed this colossal debt by colonizing both past and future, drawing energy, chemical fertilizer, and pesticides from the planet's fossil carbon, and throwing the consequences onto coming generations of our species and all others. Some of those species have already been bankrupted: they are extinct. Others will follow. Whether we are triggering an extinction as severe as the one that killed the dinosaurs, when three-quarters of all species were wiped out, is still to be seen. By the time the answer is clear, there could be nobody left to know it. The lesson of fallen societies is that civilization itself is a vulnerable organism, especially when it seems almighty. We are the world's top predator, and predators crash suddenly when they outgrow their prey. Every day, the odds climb higher that our ecological rampage will bring civilization down. If the resulting chaos unleashes full-scale nuclear war, it could well amount to a mass extinction, with *Homo sapiens* among the noted dead.

Awareness of our predicament is spreading, if slowly and with mixed results. The warnings of science are growing more urgent and precise, gaining wider attention and sparking grassroots movements such as Extinction Rebellion and the schoolchildren's strikes against their elders' shameful inertia: "I'll take my exams when you take action."[22] People are beginning to see the world dying before their eyes. The dwindling of birdlife in their gardens and bugs on their windshields backs up the scientists' alarm that falling insect numbers threaten "a catastrophic collapse of nature's ecosystems."[23] Effective reform will take political will at world level. As the Intergovernmental Panel on Climate Change (IPCC) says in its October 2018 report, keeping global warming below 1.5 degrees "is possible within the laws of chemistry and physics" but will require "unprecedented changes" before 2030.[24] Conservation and environmentalism have had some success, a few species have been pulled back from the brink, a few Green politicians have been elected, a few promising fixes (renewable energy, electric cars, etc.) are being developed. Yet at this writing, the frenzy of extraction, consumption, and destruction is still gathering speed, driven by the delusion of endless growth and the willingness of corporations to set financial profit above life itself.[25] Governments everywhere are captured by Big Oil and big money. Even parties winning office on a platform of enlightened reform have quickly bowed to vested interests. And even if fossil energy were replaced at once by clean sources, our other problems — overpopulation, overconsumption, erosion, deforestation, and accumulating waste — would still remain.

The failure of democratically elected governments to stand up for the greater good over the long run is fuelling disillusionment with democracy itself, above all among the young. Since neoliberalism took hold in the 1980s, power and money have ebbed from governments and flowed to corporations. Much of the top talent has followed that tide, draining prestige and expertise from public life. Corruptibility, low calibre, and sheer incompetence are the hallmarks of too many so-called leaders. Meanwhile, a revolt against taxation by the wealthy and by corporations, ever threatening to take their business to more "tax competitive" regimes, is resulting in decay of conservation measures, public education, civic values, and the social safety net.[26] Big Tech corporations such as Apple, Google, and Facebook have amassed vast fortunes by finessing a cloud-like, non-territorial status, evading their fair share of tax through jurisdictional sleight of hand. And these are just the quasi-lawful ways of dodging social responsibility.

There is something badly wrong with an economic regime in which twenty-six individuals own as much as half the world's population.[27] Such extreme disparity has never been seen before, not even in the days of the pharaohs or pre-Revolutionary France. Back in Classical Greece, Plato suggested that in a just society there should be no more than a 5:1 spread in income between richest and poorest. That was a hard sell then, and still would be. But what might be reasonable today? Where should the balance be struck to help the weakest while rewarding effort and achievement? Given the seriousness of what we face, this is a conversation we must have. The wealth already wrenched from nature might just be enough to buy us a lasting future if it were shared, managed, and ploughed into solutions. Inequality is the main driver behind rising population and consumption. The highest birthrates are in the poorest places, mainly Africa and the Indian subcontinent. At the other end of the see-saw, obscene wealth — the kind which owns mansions around the world and gigantic yachts with helicopter pads — has a colossal footprint, while its undue influence amounts to a dark tyranny.[28] A new yet significant part of that influence is wielded by the IT and social media industry, which in little more than a decade has not only evaded regulation but hollowed out professional journalism, invaded privacy, and grown fat by pushing a new opium of the people: an algorithmic brew of ceaseless distraction, interruption, titillation, and tailored propaganda that threatens to lock us inside a virtual present uncoupled from reality and truth.[29]

A Short History of Progress ends with the words: "Now is our last chance to get the future right." I'm reluctant to give odds that we'll do so. My level of hope fluctuates, affected by events and doubtless by the moods of my apelike mind. Nobody's odds can be more than a guess, however well informed. Wild cards could upset the table at any time: a financial crash might stop the wheels turning; a pandemic could thin us out. Conceivably, such ills might give us time by lowering pressure on the natural world. But the misery they would inflict on billions is never to be wished for and could easily unleash chaos.

In 2004, while President Bush made a foolish war in the Middle East his top priority, it was hard to be optimistic that humankind would tackle its deeper problems. Our chances, I felt, were slipping below one in two. Yet with the election of Barack Obama in 2008, expectations rose that the USA would become a helper, not a wrecker, on the world stage. Despite many disappointments, real progress on the environment was made, culminating in the 2015 Paris Agreement on global warming. At that time, I felt the odds were rising, maybe to two in three.

Since then, the postwar world we have known has gone awry. The very idea of international co-operation has come under attack — just when it is needed most. The United Nations is sidelined and vilified. Demagoguery, extremism, and polarization are on the rise, not least in the Americas. The presidents of the United States and Brazil have both declared open season on the environment from Alaska to Arizona and the Amazon, rolling back protections already in place and withdrawing from the Paris Agreement. The European Union, the world's flawed but only working alternative to balkanism and imperialism, faces upheaval within and attacks from everywhere: in the street, in opulent boardrooms, in the White House.

Often when I read the news these days, I feel I've

awakened in a dystopia I foretold, not yet in the jungled ruins of London but well on the way there. Perhaps our odds have fallen to one in three. So yes, I am less hopeful than I was in 2004. But I still have hope. Giving up in despair is a self-fulfilling prophecy. Even if the chance of success is only one in ten, it is still worth fighting for. And if we fail to act, nature will do so with the rough justice she serves on those who are too many and who take too much.

I

GAUGUIN'S QUESTIONS

THE FRENCH PAINTER and writer Paul Gauguin — by most accounts mad, bad, and dangerous to know — suffered acutely from cosmological vertigo induced by the work of Darwin and other Victorian scientists.

In the 1890s, Gauguin ran away from Paris, family, and stockbroking career to paint (and bed) native girls in the tropics. Like many a troubled soul, he could not escape so easily from himself, despite great efforts to do so with the help of drink and opium. At the bottom of his disquiet lay a longing to find what he called the "savage" — primordial man (and woman), humanity in the raw, the elusive essence of our kind. This quest eventually drew him to Tahiti and other South Sea islands, where traces of a pre-contact world — an unfallen world, in his eyes — lingered beneath the cross and *tricolore*.

In 1897, a mail steamer docked at Tahiti bringing terrible news. Gauguin's favourite child, Aline, had died suddenly from pneumonia. After months of illness, poverty, and suicidal despair, the artist harnessed his grief to produce a vast painting — more a mural in conception than a canvas[1] — in which, like the Victorian age itself, he demanded new answers to the riddle of existence. He wrote the title boldly on the image: three childlike questions, simple yet profound. *"D'Où Venons Nous? Que Sommes Nous? Où Allons Nous?"* Where do we come from? What are we? Where are we going?

The work is a sprawling panorama of enigmatic figures amid scenery that might be the groves of heathen Tahiti or an unruly Garden of Eden: worshippers or gods; cats, birds, a resting goat; a great idol with a serene expression and uplifted hands seeming to point at the beyond; a central figure plucking fruit; an Eve, the mother of mankind, who is not a voluptuous innocent like other women in Gauguin's work but a withered hag with a piercing eye inspired by a Peruvian mummy. Another figure turns in amazement to a young human pair who, as the artist wrote, "dare to consider their destiny."[2]

Gauguin's third question — Where are we going? — is what I want to address in this book. It may seem unanswerable. Who can foretell the human course through time? But I think we *can* answer it, in broad strokes, by answering the other two questions first. If we see clearly what we are and what we have done, we can recognize human behaviour that persists through many times and cultures. Knowing this can tell us what we are *likely* to do, where we are likely to go from here.

Our civilization, which subsumes most of its predecessors, is a great ship steaming at speed into the future. It travels faster, further, and more laden than any before. We may not be able to foresee every reef and hazard, but by reading her compass bearing and headway, by understanding her design, her safety record, and the abilities of her crew, we can, I think, plot a wise course between the narrows and bergs looming ahead.

And I believe we *must* do this without delay, because there are too many shipwrecks behind us. The vessel we are now aboard is not merely the biggest of all time; it is also the only one left. The future of everything we have accomplished since our intelligence evolved will depend on the wisdom of our actions over the next few years. Like all creatures, humans have made their way in the world so far by trial and error; unlike other creatures, we have a presence so colossal that error is a luxury we can no longer afford. The world has grown too small to forgive us any big mistakes.

Despite certain events of the twentieth century, most people in the Western cultural tradition still believe in the Victorian ideal of progress, a belief succinctly defined by the historian Sidney Pollard in 1968 as "the assumption that a pattern of change exists in the history of mankind . . . that it consists of irreversible changes in one direction only, and that this direction is towards improvement."[3] The very appearance on earth of creatures who can frame such a thought suggests that progress is a law of nature: the mammal is swifter than the reptile, the ape subtler than the ox, and man the cleverest of all. Our technological culture measures human progress by technology: the club is better than the fist, the arrow better than the club, the bullet better than the arrow. We came to this belief for empirical reasons: because it delivered.

Pollard notes that the idea of material progress is a very recent one — "significant only in the past three hundred years or so"[4] — coinciding closely with the rise of science and industry and the corresponding decline of traditional beliefs.[5] We no longer give much thought to moral progress — a prime concern of earlier times — except to assume that it goes hand in hand with the material. Civilized people, we tend to think, not only smell better but behave better than barbarians or savages. This notion has trouble standing up in the court of history, and I shall return to it in the next chapter when considering what is meant by "civilization."

Our practical faith in progress has ramified and hardened into an ideology — a secular religion which, like the religions that progress has challenged, is blind to certain flaws in its credentials. Progress, therefore, has become "myth" in the anthropological sense. By this I do not mean a belief that is flimsy or untrue. Successful myths are powerful and often partly true. As I've written elsewhere: "Myth is an arrangement of the past, whether real or imagined, in patterns that reinforce a culture's deepest values and aspirations. . . . Myths are so fraught with meaning that we live and die by them. They are the maps by which cultures navigate through time."[6]

The myth of progress has sometimes served us well — those of us seated at the best tables, anyway — and may continue to do so. But I shall argue in this book that it has also become dangerous. Progress has an internal logic that can lead beyond reason to catastrophe. A seductive trail of successes may end in a trap.

Take weapons, for example. Ever since the Chinese invented gunpowder, there has been great progress in the making of bangs: from the firecracker to the cannon, from the petard to the high explosive shell. And just when high explosives were reaching a state of perfection, progress found the infinitely bigger bang in the atom. But when the bang we can make can blow up our world, we have made rather too much progress.

Several of the scientists who created the atomic bomb recognized this in the 1940s, telling politicians and others that the new weapons had to be destroyed. "The unleashed power of the atom has changed everything save our modes of thinking," Albert Einstein wrote, "and we thus drift toward unparalleled catastrophes." And a few years later, President Kennedy said, "If mankind does not put an end to war, war will put an end to mankind."

When I was a boy, in the 1950s, the shadow of too much progress in weaponry— of Hiroshima, Nagasaki, and vaporized Pacific islands   had already fallen over the world. It has now darkened our lives for about sixty years, and so much has been said on the subject that I needn't add more.[7] My point here is that weapons technology was merely the first area of human progress to reach an impasse by threatening to destroy the planet on which it developed.

At the time, this progress trap was seen as an aberration. In all other fields, including those of nuclear power and chemical pesticides, the general faith in progress was largely unshaken. Advertisements of the 1950s showed a smiling "Mrs. 1970," who, having bought the right brand of vacuum cleaner, was enjoying the future in advance. Each year's motor car looked different from the previous year's (especially if it wasn't). "Bigger! Wider! Longer!" sang the girls in a jingle, automakers being keen, then as now, to sell bigger as better. And peasants were freed from vermin with generous dustings of DDT in what became known as the Third World — that unravelling tapestry of non-Western cultures seen as a relic of "backwardness" torn between the superpowers. In both its capitalist and communist versions, the great promise of modernity was progress without limit and without end.

The collapse of the Soviet Union led many to conclude that there was really only one way of progress after all. In 1992 Francis Fukuyama, a former U.S. State Department official, declared that capitalism and democracy were the "end" of history — not only its destination but its goal.[8] Doubters pointed out that capitalism and democracy are not necessarily bedfellows, citing Nazi Germany, modern China, and the worldwide archipelago of sweatshop tyrannies. Yet Fukuyama's naive triumphalism strengthened a belief, mainly on the political right, that those who have not chosen the true way forward should be made to do so for their own good — by force, if necessary. In this respect, and in the self-interest it obscures, the current ideology of progress resembles the missionary projects of past empires, whether seventh-century Islam, sixteenth-century Spain, or nineteenth-century Britain.

Since the Cold War ended, we have held the nuclear genie at bay but have not begun to stuff it back in its bottle. Yet we are busy unleashing other powerful forces — cybernetics, biotechnology, nanotechnology — that we hope will be good tools, but whose consequences we cannot foresee.

The most immediate threat, however, may be nothing more glamorous than our own waste. Like most problems with technology, pollution is a problem of scale. The biosphere might have been able to tolerate our dirty old friends coal and oil if we'd burned them gradually. But how long can it withstand a blaze of consumption so frenzied that the dark side of this planet glows like a fanned ember in the night of space?

Alexander Pope said, rather snobbishly, that a little learning is a dangerous thing; Thomas Huxley later asked, "Where is the man who has so much as to be out of danger?"[9] Technology is addictive. Material progress creates problems that are — or seem to be — soluble only by further progress. Again, the devil here is in the scale: a good bang can be useful; a better bang can end the world.

So far I have spoken of such problems as if they were purely modern, arising from industrial technologies. But while progress strong enough to destroy the world is indeed modern, the devil of scale who transforms benefits into traps has plagued us since the Stone Age. This devil lives within us and gets out whenever we steal a march on nature, tipping the balance between cleverness and recklessness, between need and greed.

Palaeolithic hunters who learnt how to kill two mammoths instead of one had made progress. Those who learnt how to kill 200 — by driving a whole herd over a cliff — had made too much. They lived high for a while, then starved.

Many of the great ruins that grace the deserts and jungles of the earth are monuments to progress traps, the headstones of civilizations which fell victim to their own success. In the fates of such societies — once mighty, complex, and brilliant — lie the most instructive lessons for our own. Their ruins are shipwrecks that mark the shoals of progress. Or — to use a more modern analogy — they are fallen airliners whose black boxes can tell us what went wrong. In this book, I want to read some of these boxes in the hope that we can avoid repeating past mistakes, of flight plan, crew selection, and design. Of course, our civilization's particulars differ from those of previous ones. But not as much as we like to think. All cultures, past and present, are dynamic. Even the most slow-moving were, in the long run, works in progress. While the facts of each case differ, the patterns through time are alarmingly — and encouragingly — similar. We should be alarmed by the predictability of our mistakes but encouraged that this very fact makes them useful for understanding what we face today.

Like Gauguin, we often prefer to think of the deep past as innocent and unspoiled, a time of ease and simple plenty before a fall from paradise. The words "Eden" and "Paradise" feature prominently in the titles of popular books on anthropology and history. For some, Eden was the pre-agricultural world, the age of hunting and gathering; for others, it was the pre-Columbian world, the Americas before the white man; and for many, it was the pre-industrial world, the long stillness before the machine. Certainly there have been good and bad times to be alive. But the truth is that human beings drove themselves out of Eden, and they have done it again and again by fouling their own nests. If we want to live in an earthly paradise, it is up to us to shape it, share it, and look after it.

In pondering his first question — Where do we come from? — Gauguin might have agreed with G. K. Chesterton, who remarked, "Man is an exception, whatever else he is. . . . If it is not true that a divine being fell, then we can only say that one of the animals went entirely off its head."[10] We now know much more about that 5-million-year process of an ape going off its head, so it is hard, today, to recapture the shock felt around the world when the implications of evolutionary theory first became clear.

Writing in 1600, Shakespeare had Hamlet exclaim, "What a piece of work is a man! How noble in reason! how infinite in faculty! . . . in action how like an angel! in apprehension how like a god!"[11] His audience would have shared Hamlet's mix of wonder, scorn, and irony at human nature. But very few, if any, would have doubted that they were made as the Bible told: "And God said, Let us make man in our image, after our likeness."

They were prepared to overlook theological rough spots posed by sex, race, and colour. Was God black or blond? Did he have a navel? And what about the rest of his physical equipment? Such things didn't bear thinking about too closely. Our kinship with apes, which seems so obvious now, was unsuspected; apes were seen (if seen, which was rarely in Europe in those days) as parodies of man, not cousins or possible forebears.

If they thought about it at all, most people of 1600 believed that what we now call scientific method would simply open and illuminate the great clockwork set in place by Providence, as God saw fit to let humans share in admiration of his handiwork. Galileo's troubling thoughts about the structure of the heavens were an unexploded bomb, unproven and unassimilated. (Hamlet still subscribes to a pre-Copernican universe, a "brave o'erhanging firmament.") The inevitable collision between scriptural faith and empirical evidence was barely guessed at. Most of the really big surprises — the age of the earth, the origin of animals and man, the shape and scale of the heavens — still lay ahead. Most people of 1600 were far more alarmed by priests and witches than by natural philosophers, though the lines between these three were often unclear.

From the biblical definition of man, and the common-sense principle that it takes one to know one, Hamlet thinks he knows what a human being is, and most

Westerners continued to think they knew what they were for another 200 years. The rot of rational doubt on the matter of our beginnings did not set in until the nineteenth century, when geologists realized that the chronology in the Bible could not account for the antiquity they read in rocks, fossils, and sediments. Some civilizations, notably the Maya and the Hindu, assumed that time was vast or infinite, but ours always had a petty notion of its scale. "The poor world is almost six thousand years old," sighs Rosalind in *As You Like It*,[12] a typical estimate derived from the patriarchal lifetimes, "begats," and other clues in the Old Testament. Half a century after Rosalind's sigh, Archbishop Ussher of Armagh and his contemporary John Lightfoot took it upon themselves to pinpoint the very moment of Creation. "Man was created by the Trinity," Lightfoot declared, "on October 23, 4004 B.C., at nine o'clock in the morning."[13]

Such precision was new, but the idea of a young earth had always been essential to the Judaeo-Christian view of time as teleological — a short one-way trip from Creation to Judgment, from Adam to Doom. Newton and other thinkers began to voice doubts about this on theoretical grounds, but they had no real evidence or means of testing their ideas. Then, in the 1830s, while the young Charles Darwin was sailing round the world aboard the *Beagle*, Charles Lyell published his *Principles of Geology*, arguing that the earth transformed itself gradually, by processes still at work, and might therefore be as old as Newton had proposed — some ten times older than the Bible allowed.[14]

Under Queen Victoria, the earth aged quickly — by many millions of years in decades — enough to make room for Darwin's evolutionary mechanism and the growing collection of giant lizards and lowbrowed fossil humans being dug up around the world and put on show in South Kensington and the Crystal Palace.[15]

In 1863, Lyell brought out a book called *Geological Evidences of the Antiquity of Man*, and in 1871 (twelve years after his *Origin of Species*), Darwin published *The Descent of Man*. Their ideas were spread by enthusiastic popularizers, above all Thomas Huxley, famous for saying, in a debate on evolution with Bishop Wilberforce, that he would rather acknowledge an ape for his grandfather than be a clergyman careless with the truth.[16] Hamlet's exclamation therefore became a question: What exactly *is* a man? Like children who reach an age when they're no longer satisfied that a stork brought them into the world, a newly educated public began to doubt the old mythology.

By the time Gauguin was painting his masterpiece at the end of the century, the first two of his questions were getting concrete answers. His compatriot Madame Curie and others working on radioactivity were uncovering nature's timekeepers: elements in rock that break down at a measurable rate. By 1907, the physicists Boltwood and Rutherford could show that the earth's age is reckoned not in millions of years but in billions.[17] Archaeology showed that the genus *Homo* was a latecomer, even among mammals, taking shape long after early pigs, cats, and elephants began walking the earth (or, in the case of whales, gave up walking and went swimming). "Man," wrote H. G. Wells, "is a mere upstart."[18]

What was extraordinary about human development — the one big thing that set us apart from other creatures — was that we "leveraged" natural evolution by developing cultures transmissible through speech from one generation to the next. "The human word," Northrop Frye wrote in another context, "is the power that orders our chaos."[19] The effect of this power was unprecedented, allowing complex tools, weapons, and elaborate planned behaviours. Even very simple technology had enormous consequences. Basic clothing and built shelter, for example, opened up every climate from the tropics to the tundra. We moved beyond the environments that had made us, and began to make *ourselves*.

Though we became experimental creatures of our own devising, it's important to bear in mind that we had no inkling of this process, let alone its consequences, until only the last six or seven of our 100,000 generations. We have done it all sleepwalking. Nature let a few apes into the lab of evolution, switched on the lights, and left us there to mess about with an ever-growing supply of ingredients and processes. The effect on us and the world has accumulated ever since. Let's list a few steps between the earliest times and this: sharp stones, animal skins, useful bits of bone and wood, wild fire, tame fire, seeds for eating, seeds for planting, houses, villages, pottery, cities, metals, wheels, explosives. What strikes one most forcefully is the acceleration, the runaway progression of change — or to put it another way, the collapsing of time.

From the first chipped stone to the first smelted iron took
nearly 3 million years; from the first iron to the hydrogen
bomb took only 3,000.

The Old Stone Age, or Palaeolithic era, lasted from the
appearance of toolmaking hominids, nearly 3 million
years ago, until the melting of the last ice age, about
12,000 years ago. It spans more than 99.5 per cent
of human existence. During most of that time, the pace
of change was so slow that entire cultural traditions
(revealed mainly by their stone tool kits) replicated
themselves, generation after generation, almost iden-
tically over staggering periods of time. It might take
100,000 years for a new style or technique to be developed; then, as culture began to ramify and feed on itself,
only 10,000; then mere thousands and centuries. Cultural change begat physical change and vice versa in a
feedback loop.

Nowadays we have reached such a pass that the skills
and mores we learn in childhood are outdated by the
time we're thirty, and few people past fifty can keep up
with their culture — whether in idiom, attitudes, taste, or
technology — even if they try. But I am getting ahead in
the story. Most people living in the Old Stone Age would
not have noticed any cultural change at all. The human
world that individuals entered at birth was the same as
the one they left at death. There was variation in events,
of course — feasts, famines, local triumphs and disasters
— but the patterns within each society must have seemed
immutable. There was just one way to do things, one

mythology, one vocabulary, one set of stories; things were just the way they were.

It is possible to imagine exceptions to what I have just said. The generation that saw the first use of fire, for instance, *was* perhaps aware that its world had changed. But we can't be sure how quickly even that Promethean discovery took hold. Most likely, fire was *used*, when available from wildfires and volcanoes, for a long time before it was *kept*. And then it was *kept* for a very long time before anyone learnt it could be *made*. Some may remember the 1981 film *Quest for Fire*, in which the lithe figure of Rae Dawn Chong scampers about in nothing but a thin layer of mud and ashes. The film was based on a novel published in 1911 by the Belgian writer J. H. Rosny.[20] Rosny's original title was *La Guerre du Feu — The War for Fire* — and the book, more than the film, explores deadly competition between various human groups to monopolize fire in much the same way that modern nations try to monopolize nuclear weapons. Throughout the hundreds of centuries when our ancestors tended a flame but could not make one, putting out their rivals' campfire in an Ice Age winter would have been a deed of mass murder.

The first taming of fire is hard to date. All we know is that people were using fire by at least half a million years ago, possibly twice that.[21] This was the time of *Homo erectus*, the "upright man," who was much like us from the neck down, but whose braincase had only about two-thirds the modern capacity. Anthropologists are still debating when *Homo erectus* first appeared and when he and she were superseded, which is largely a matter of defining that evolutionary stage. Scholars are even more divided on how well *erectus* could think and speak.

Modern apes, whose brains are much smaller than those of *erectus*, use simple tools, have wide knowledge of medicinal plants, and can recognize themselves in a mirror. Studies using non-verbal language (computer symbols, sign language, etc.) show that apes can employ a vocabulary of several hundred "words," though there is disagreement on what this ability says about ape communication in the wild. It *is* clear that different groups of the same species — for example, chimps in separate parts of Africa — have different habits and traditions, passed on to the young just as in human groups. In short, apes have the beginnings of culture. So do other intelligent creatures, such as whales, elephants, and certain birds, but no species except humankind has reached the point at which culture becomes the main driver of an evolutionary surge, outrunning environmental and physical constraints.

The bloodlines of man and ape split about 5 million years ago, and as I mentioned, hominids making crude stone tools appeared some 2 million years later. It would therefore be foolish to underestimate the skills of *Homo erectus*, who, by the time he was toasting his callused feet at a campfire half a million years ago, was nine-tenths of the way along the road from an ancestral ape to us. With the taming of fire came the first spike on the graph of human numbers. Fire would have made life much easier in many environments. Fire kept caves warm and big predators away. Cooking and smoking greatly increased the reliable food supply. Burning of undergrowth extended grazing lands for game. It is now recognized that many supposedly wild landscapes inhabited down to historic times by hunter-gatherers — the North American prairies and the Australian outback, for instance — were shaped by deliberate fire-setting.[22] "Man," wrote the great anthropologist and writer Loren Eiseley, "is himself a flame. He has burned through the animal world and appropriated its vast stores of protein for his own."[23]

About the last big thing the experts agree on is that *Homo erectus* originated in Africa, the home of all early hominids, and by a million years ago was living in several temperate and tropical zones of the "Old World," the contiguous Eurasian landmass. This is not to say the Upright Man was thick on the ground, even after he tamed fire. Perhaps fewer than 100,000 people, scattered in family bands, were all that stood between evolutionary failure and the 6 billion of us here today.[24]

After *Homo erectus* the evolutionary path gets muddy, trodden into a mire by rival tribes of anthropologists. One camp, that of the "multiregional" hypothesis, sees *Homo erectus* evolving by fits and starts into modern humanity wherever he happened to be through gene diffusion, otherwise known as mating with strangers. This view seems to fit well with many of the fossil finds but less well with some interpretations of DNA. Another camp — the "Out of Africa" school — sees most evolutionary change taking place on that continent, then erupting over the rest of the world.[25] In this second view, successive waves of new and improved humans kill off, or, at any rate, outcompete, their forerunners wherever they find them, until all the lowbrows are gone. This theory implies that each new wave of African man was a separate species, unable to breed with other descendants of the previous kind — which may be plausible if different types evolved without contact for long periods but is less likely over shorter spans of time.[26]

The debate over the path of human progress gets most heated when we reach our controversial cousins, the Neanderthals. These lived mainly in Europe and north-west Asia in quite recent times — well within the last one-twentieth of the human journey. A Neanderthal Gauguin, thawed out from a receding glacier today, might wake up and ask, "Who were we? Where did we come from? Where did we go?" The answers would depend on whom he approached. Experts cannot even agree on his scientific name.

In round figures, Neanderthals appear about 130,000 years ago and disappear about 100,000 years later. Their "arrival" date is less certain than their departure, but it seems they evolved at about the same time as early examples of what is thought to be our modern kind — often called Cro-Magnon, after a rockshelter in the lovely Dordogne region of southern France, where the human fossil record is the richest in the world.

Ever since they were first identified, Neanderthals have been the butt of what I call "palaeo-racism," lampooned as cartoon cavemen, a subhuman, knuckle-dragging breed. H. G. Wells called them the "Grisly Folk" and made an unflattering guess at how they might have looked: "an extreme hairiness, an ugliness . . . a repulsive strangeness in his . . . low forehead, his beetle brows, his ape neck, and his inferior stature."[27] Many have claimed that Neanderthals were cannibals, which could be true, for so are we — later humans have a long record of cannibalism, right down to modern times.[28]

The first Neanderthal skeleton was unearthed in 1856 from a cave in a valley near Düsseldorf, Germany. The place had been named after the composer Joachim Neumann, who had rather affectedly rendered his surname into Greek as "Neander." Englished, Neanderthal is simply "Newmandale." Fitting enough: a new man had indeed come to light in the dale, a new man at least 30,000 years old. Not that Neanderthal Man's seniority was recognized immediately. The French, noting the skull's thickness, were inclined to think it had belonged to a German. The Germans said it was most likely from a Slav, a Cossack mercenary who had crawled into the cave and died.[29] But just three years later, in 1859, two things happened: Darwin published *On the Origin of Species* and Charles Lyell, visiting the gravels of the River Somme (to become infamous, not sixty years later, as a human slaughterhouse), recognized chipped flints as weapons from the Ice Age.

Once the scientists of the day had acknowledged that the Neanderthaler wasn't a Cossack, they cast him in the newly minted role of the "missing link" — that elusive creature loping halfway across the evolutionary page

between an ape and us. The New Man became the right
man at the right time, the one who, "in his glowering
silence and mystery, would show . . . the unthinkable:
that humans were animals."[30] It was assumed that he
had little or no power of speech, ran like a baboon, and
walked on the outsides of his feet. But as more bones
were unearthed and analysed, this view did not stand up.
The most "apelike" skeletons were found to be sufferers
from osteoarthritis, severely crippled individuals who
had evidently been supported for years by their commu-
nity. Evidence also came to light that the "grisly folk" had
not only cared for their sick but also buried their dead
with religious rites — with flowers and ochre and animal
horns — the first people on earth known to do so. And
last but not least, the Neanderthal brain turned out to be
bigger than our own. Perhaps *Homo neanderthalensis* was
really not so brutish after all. Perhaps he deserved to be
promoted to a subspecies of modern man: *Homo sapiens
neanderthalensis*. And if that were so, the two variants
could, by definition, have interbred.[31]

Before the two began to compete in Europe, the
Cro-Magnons lived south of the Mediterranean and the
Neanderthals north. Then as now, the Middle East was a
crossroads. Dwelling sites in that turbulent region show
occupation by both Neanderthals and Cro-Magnons
beginning about 100,000 years ago. We can't tell whether
they ever lived there at exactly the same times, let alone
whether they shared the Holy Land harmoniously.
Most likely their arrangement was a kind of time-share,
with Neanderthals moving south out of Europe during

especially cold spells in the Ice Age and Cro-Magnons moving north from Africa whenever the climate warmed. What is most interesting is that the material culture of the two groups, as shown by their artefacts, was identical over a span of more than 50,000 years. Archaeologists find it difficult to say whether any given cave was occupied by Neanderthals or Cro-Magnons unless human bone is found with the tools. I take this as strong evidence that the two groups had very similar mental and linguistic capabilities, that neither was more primitive or "less evolved."

No Neanderthal flesh, skin, or hair has yet come to light, so we can't say whether these people were brown or blond, hairy as Esau or smooth as Jacob. Nor do we know much about the Cro-Magnons' superficial appearance, though genetic studies suggest that most modern Europeans may be descended from them.[32] We know these populations only by their bones. Both were roughly the same height, between five and six feet tall with the usual variation between sexes. But one was built for strength and the other for speed. The Neanderthal was heavyset and brawny, like a professional weightlifter or wrestler. The Cro-Magnon was slighter and more gracile, a track athlete rather than a bodybuilder. It is hard to know how far these differences were innate, and how much they reflected habitat and lifestyle. In 1939, the anthropologist Carleton Coon drew an amusing reconstruction of a Neanderthal cleaned up, shaved, and dressed in a fedora, jacket, and tie. Such a man, Coon remarked, might pass unnoticed on the New York subway.

As such analogies suggest, the variation between Neanderthal and Cro-Magnon skeletons does not fall far outside the range of modern humans. Put side by side, the bony remains of Arnold Schwarzenegger and Woody Allen might exhibit a similar contrast. The skull, however, is another matter. The so-called classic Neanderthal (which is a rather misleading term because it is self-fulfilling, based on the more pronounced examples) had a long, low skull with strong brow ridges in front and a bony ledge across the nape of the neck, the Neanderthal "bun" or "chignon." The jaw was robust, with strong teeth and a rounded chin; the nose was broad and presumably squat. At first glance the design looks archaic, much the same architecture as that of *Homo erectus*. But — as noted — the Neanderthal brain was bigger on average than the Cro-Magnon. Coon's subway rider had a thick skull but not necessarily a thick head.

What this adds up to, I think, is that the supposedly archaic characteristics of the Neanderthal were in fact an overlay of cold-climate adaptations on an essentially modern human frame.[33] The high foreheads of modern people can get so chilled that the brain is damaged, and icy air can freeze the lungs. The Neanderthal brain was sheltered by the massive brows and the low, yet roomy, vault. Air entering Neanderthal lungs was warmed by the broad nose, and the whole face had a better blood supply. Thickset, brawny people do not lose body heat as quickly as slender people. Signs of similar adaptation (in body shape, at least) can be seen among modern Inuit, Andeans, and Himalayans — and this after only a few thousand years of living with intense cold, beside the 100,000 during which Europe's Neanderthals made their living on the front lines of the Ice Age.

Things seem to have gone well enough for them until Cro-Magnons began moving north and west from the Middle East, about 40,000 years ago. Until then, the cold had been the Neanderthals' great ally, always turning invaders back sooner or later, like the Russian winter. But this time the Cro-Magnons came to stay. The invasion seems to have coincided with climatic instability linked to sudden reversals of ocean currents that caused freezing and thawing of the North Atlantic in upsets as short as a decade.[34] Such sharp changes — severe as the worst predictions we now have for global warming — would have devastated animal and plant communities on which the Neanderthals depended. We know that they ate a lot of big game, which they hunted by ambush — breaks in their bones are similar to those sustained by rodeo cowboys, showing they went in close for the kill. And we know that they were not usually nomadic, occupying the same caves and valleys year-round. Humans in general have been called a "weed species," thriving in disrupted environments, but of these two groups, the Neanderthals were the more rooted. The Cro-Magnons were the invasive briars. Climate change would have made life difficult for everyone, of course, but unstable conditions could have given the edge to the less physically specialized, weaker at close quarters but quicker on their feet.

I remember seeing a cartoon when I was a schoolboy — I think it may have been in *Punch* — showing three or four bratty Neanderthal children standing on a cliff, badgering their father: "Daddy, Daddy! Can we go and throw rocks at the Cro-Magnons today?" For about ten millennia, from 40,000 to 30,000 years ago, the late Neanderthals and the early Cro-Magnons probably did throw rocks at each other, not to mention dousing camp-fires, stealing game, and perhaps seizing women and children. At the end of that unimaginably long struggle, Europe and the whole world belonged to our kind, and the "classic" Neanderthal was gone forever. But what really happened? Did the Neanderthal line die out, or was it to some degree assimilated?

The 10,000-year struggle was so gradual that it may have been scarcely perceptible — a fitful, inconclusive war with land lost and won at the rate of a few miles in a lifetime. Yet, like all wars, it sparked innovation. New tools and weapons appeared, new clothing and rituals, the beginnings of cave painting (an art form that would reach its height during the last great fling of the Ice Age, after the classic Neanderthals had gone). We also know that cultural contact went both ways. Late Neanderthal sites in France show change and adaptation at a pace never seen before.[35] By then, near the end, the war's impli-cations must have become dreadfully clear. It seems that the last Neanderthal bands held out in the mountains of Spain and Yugoslavia, driven like Apaches into rougher and rougher terrain.

If the warfare picture I have sketched has any truth to it, then we face unpalatable conclusions. This is what makes the Neanderthal debate so emotional: it is not only about ancient people but about ourselves. If it turns out that the Neanderthals disappeared because they were an evolutionary dead end, we can merely shrug and blame natural selection for their fate. But if they were in fact a variant or race of modern man, then we must admit to ourselves that their death may have been the first genocide. Or, worse, *not* the first — merely the first of which evidence survives. It may follow from this that we are descended from a million years of ruthless victories, genetically predisposed by the sins of our fathers to do likewise again and again. As the anthropologist Milford Wolpoff has written on this period: "You can't imagine one human population replacing another except through violence."[36] No, you can't — especially on the blood-stained earth of Europe, amid Stone Age forebodings of the final solution and the slaughter of the Somme.

In the aftermath of the Second World War, William Golding explored ancient genocide in his extraordinary novel *The Inheritors*. With wonderful assurance, Golding takes the reader inside the minds of an unnamed group of early humans. The book's epigraph, from Wells, invokes Neanderthals, though the anthropological specifics fit better with much earlier stages of mankind. Golding's folk are gentle, naive, chimp-like woodland dwellers. They eat no meat except the leavings of big predators; they are poor speakers, using telepathy as much as language; they have fire but few weapons, and have never suspected there is anyone else in the world except themselves.

Yet Golding's anachronisms don't matter: his people may not fit any particular set of bones from the real past, but they stand for many. In the course of a few spring days, the forest dwellers are invaded for the first time by people like us, who with their boats, bonfires, arrows, raucous voices, wholesale tree-felling, and drunken orgies baffle and fascinate the "forest devils" even as they kill them one by one. At the end, only a mewling baby remains, kept by a woman who has lost her own child to drain the milk from her breasts. The invaders then move on through the new land, their leader plotting further murders — murders now amongst themselves — as he sharpens a weapon, "a point against the darkness of the world."

Golding had no doubt that the ruthless were the winners of prehistory, but another question he raised is still unsettled: Does any Neanderthal blood flow in modern humans? How likely is it that during 10,000 years of interaction, there was no sex, unconsensual though it may have been? And if there was sex, were there children? DNA studies on Neanderthal remains have been inconclusive so far.[37] But the skeleton of a child found recently in Portugal strongly suggests interbreeding, as do bones from Croatia and elsewhere in the Balkans.[38]

I also have personal evidence that Neanderthal genes may still be with us. A few modern people have telltale ridges on their heads.[39] I happen to have one — a bony shelf across the back of the skull that looks and feels like the Neanderthal bun. So until new findings come along to settle the matter, I choose to believe that Neanderthal blood still flows, however faint, in the Cro-Magnon tide.[40]

* * *

Despite the many details of our ancestry still to be worked out, the twentieth century *has* broadly answered the first two of Gauguin's questions. There is no room for rational doubt that we are apes, and that, regardless of our exact route through time, we come ultimately from Africa. But unlike other apes, we tamper, and are tampering more than ever, with our destiny. For a long time now, there has been no such thing as that Enlightenment wild goose which Gauguin sought, the Natural Man. Like those arthritic Neanderthals who were cared for by their families, we cannot live without our cultures. We have met the maker of Hamlet's "piece of work" — and it is us.

II

THE GREAT EXPERIMENT

SOMEONE FOND OF logical absurdities once defined specialists as "people who know more and more about less and less, until they know all about nothing." Many animals are highly specialized, their bodies adapted to specific ecological niches and ways of life. Specialization brings short-term rewards but can lead, in the long run, to an evolutionary dead end. When the prey of the sabre-toothed cat died out, so did the cat.

The modern human animal — our physical being — is a generalist. We have no fangs, claws, or venom built into our bodies. Instead we've devised tools and weapons — knives, spearheads, poisoned arrows. Elementary inventions such as warm clothing and simple watercraft allowed us to overrun the whole planet before the end of the last ice age.[1] Our specialization is the brain. The flexibility of the brain's interactions with nature, through culture, has been the key to our success.

Cultures can adapt far more quickly than genes to new threats and needs.

But as I suggested in the previous chapter, there is still a risk. As cultures grow more elaborate, and technologies more powerful, they themselves may become ponderous specializations — vulnerable and, in extreme cases, deadly. The atomic bomb, a logical progression from the arrow and the bullet, became the first technology to threaten our whole species with extinction. It is what I call a "progress trap." But much simpler technologies have also seduced and ruined societies in the past, even back in the Stone Age.

In the previous chapter, I raised three questions asked by Paul Gauguin in his great 1897 painting, entitled, *Where Do We Come From? What Are We? Where Are We Going?* At a practical level, anthropology has answered the first two: we now know that we are the remote descendants of apes who lived in Africa about 5 million years ago. Modern apes, which are also descended from the same original stock, are kin, not ancestors. Our main difference from chimps and gorillas is that over the last 3 million years or so, we have been shaped less and less by nature, and more and more by culture. We have become experimental creatures of our own making.

This experiment has never been tried before. And we, its unwitting authors, have never controlled it. The experiment is now moving very quickly and on a colossal scale. Since the early 1900s, the world's population has multiplied by four and its economy — a rough measure of the human load on nature — by more than forty. We have reached a stage where we must bring the experiment under rational control, and guard against present and potential dangers. It's entirely up to us. If we fail — if we blow up or degrade the biosphere so it can no longer sustain us — nature will merely shrug and conclude that letting apes run the laboratory was fun for a while but in the end a bad idea.

We have already caused so many extinctions that our dominion over the earth will appear in the fossil record like the impact of an asteroid. So far, we are only a small asteroid compared with the one that clobbered the dinosaurs.[2] But if the extinctions continue much longer, or if we unleash weapons of mass destruction — I mean the real ones kept in huge stockpiles by the great powers — then the next layer of fossils will indeed show a major hiatus in this planet's life.

I suggested in the previous chapter that prehistory, like history, tells us that the nice folk didn't win, that we are at best the heirs of many ruthless victories and at worst the heirs of genocide. We may well be descended from humans who repeatedly exterminated rival humans — culminating in the suspicious death of our Neanderthal cousins some 30,000 years ago. Whatever the truth of that event, it marks the beginning of the Upper Palaeolithic period — the last and briefest of three divisions in the Old Stone Age, about one-hundredth of the whole.

In this chapter I want to see what we can deduce from the first progress trap — the perfection of hunting, which ended the Old Stone Age — and how our escape from that trap by the invention of farming led to our greatest experiment: worldwide civilization. We then have to ask ourselves this urgent question: Could civilization itself be another and much greater trap?

The Old Stone Age began nearly 3 million years ago, with the first rough tools made by the first rough beasts slouching towards humanity, and ended only 12,000 years ago, when the great ice sheets withdrew for the last time to the poles and ranges where they await further climate change. Geologically speaking, 3 million years is only a wink, one minute of earth's day. But in human terms, the Old Stone Age is a deep abyss of time — more than 99.5 per cent of our existence — from which we crawled into the soft beds of civilization only yesterday.

Even our modern subspecies, *Homo sapiens sapiens*, is between ten and twenty times older than the oldest civilization. But measured as subjective human experience — as a sum of individual lives — more people have lived a civilized life than any other.[3] Civilization does not run deep in time, but it runs wide, for it is both the cause and the effect of a population boom that has yet to level off.

I should make it clear that I'm defining "civilization" and "culture" in a technical, anthropological way. By culture I mean the whole of any society's knowledge, beliefs, and practices. Culture is everything: from veganism to cannibalism; Beethoven, Botticelli, and body piercing; what you do in the bedroom, the bathroom, and the church of your choice (if your culture allows a choice); and all of technology from the split stone to the split atom. Civilizations are a specific kind of culture: large, complex societies based on the domestication of plants, animals, and human beings.[4] Civilizations vary in their makeup but typically have towns, cities, governments, social classes, and specialized professions. All civilizations are cultures, or conglomerates of cultures, but not all cultures are civilizations.

Archaeologists generally agree that the first civilizations were those of Sumer — in southern Mesopotamia, or what is now Iraq — and Egypt, both emerging about 3000 B.C. By 1000 B.C., civilization ringed the world, notably in India, China, Mexico, Peru, and parts of Europe.

From ancient times until today, civilized people have believed they behave better, and *are* better, than so-called savages. But the moral values attached to civilization are specious: too often used to justify attacking and dominating other, less powerful, societies. In their imperial heyday, the French had their "civilizing mission" and the British their "white man's burden" — the bearing of which was eased by automatic weapons. As Hilaire Belloc wrote in 1898: "Whatever happens, we have got / The Maxim gun, and they have not." Nowadays, Washington claims to lead and safeguard "the civilized world," a tradition in American rhetoric that began with the uprooting and exterminating of that country's first inhabitants.[5]

The Roman circus, the Aztec sacrifices, the Inquisition bonfires, the Nazi death camps — all have been the work of highly civilized societies.[6] In the twentieth century alone, at least 100 million people, mostly civilians, died in wars.[7] Savages have done no worse. At the gates of the Colosseum and the concentration camp, we have no choice but to abandon hope that civilization is, in itself, a guarantor of moral progress.

When Mahatma Gandhi came to England in the 1930s for talks on Indian self-rule, a reporter asked him what he thought of Western civilization. Gandhi, who had just visited the London slums, replied: "I think it would be a very good idea."[8] If I sound at times rather hard on civilization, this is because, like Gandhi, I would like it to fulfill its promise and succeed. I would rather live in a house than in a rock-shelter. I like great buildings and good books. I like knowing that I am an ape, that the world is round, that the sun is a star and the stars are suns — taken-for-granted knowledge that took thousands of years to wrest from "chaos and old night."[9] For all its cruelties, civilization is precious, an experiment worth continuing. It is also precarious: as we climbed the ladder of progress, we kicked out the rungs below. There is no going back without catastrophe. Those who don't like civilization, and can't wait for it to fall on its arrogant face, should keep in mind that there is no other way to support humanity in anything like our present numbers or estate.[10]

The Old Stone Age now seems so remote that we seldom give it a thought, except perhaps to chuckle at a "Farside" cartoon. Yet it ended so recently — only six times further back than the birth of Christ and the Roman Empire —

that the big changes since we left the cave have all been cultural, not physical. A long-lived species like ours can't evolve significantly over so short an interval. This means that while culture and technology are cumulative, innate intelligence is not.[11]

Like the butt of Dr. Johnson's joke that much may be made of a Scotsman if he be caught young, a late-Palaeolithic child snatched from a campfire and raised among us now would have an even chance at earning a degree in astrophysics or computer science. To use a computer analogy, we are running twenty-first-century software on hardware last upgraded 50,000 years ago or more. This may explain quite a lot of what we see in the news.

Culture itself has created this uniquely human problem: partly because cultural growth runs far ahead of evolution, and because for a long time now the accreting mass of culture has forestalled natural selection and put destiny into our hands.

"I will tell you what a man is," wrote William Golding in his 1956 novel, *Pincher Martin*, which though set during the Second World War continues the meditation on humanity that he began in his Stone Age novel, *The Inheritors*: "He is a freak, an ejected foetus robbed of his natural development, thrown out in the world with a naked covering of parchment, with too little room for his teeth and a soft bulging skull like a bubble. But nature stirs a pudding there. . . ."[12]

In Golding's pudding seethe many ingredients: genius and madness, logic and belief, instinct and hallucination, compassion and cruelty, love, hate, sex, art, greed — all the drives towards life and death. In the individual, the sum of these is personality; in society, it is the collective personality called culture. In the long run, the pudding of culture has always grown in size. And there have been several yeasty times when it rose quite suddenly and spilled across the kitchen.

The first of these was the taming of fire by *Homo erectus*, which tipped the balance of survival strongly in our favour. The next, half a million years later, was the perfection of hunting by Cro-Magnons soon after they displaced the Neanderthals. New weapons were produced: lighter, sharper, longer-ranged, more elegant and deadly.[13] Bead adornment, bone carvings, musical instruments, and elaborate burials became common. Magnificent paintings appeared on cave walls and rock faces, in a vigorous naturalism that would not be seen again until the Renaissance.

Many of these things had already been done on a small scale by Neanderthals and earlier Cro-Magnons,[14] so this spurt of art and technology cannot (as some claim) be evidence that we suddenly evolved into a new species with brand-new cognitive powers. But it *is* evidence of a familiar cultural pattern: leisure born of a food surplus. The hunters and gatherers were producing more than mere subsistence, giving themselves time to paint the walls, make beads and effigies, play music, indulge in religious rituals. For the first time, people were rich.

To draw a rough analogy between two unconnected eras of very different length and complexity, there are certain resemblances between this end-time of the Old Stone Age and the past half millennium of Western "discovery" and conquest. Since A.D. 1492, one kind of civilization — the European — has largely destroyed and displaced all others, fattening and remaking itself into an industrial force in the process (a point I shall return to in a later chapter). During the Upper Palaeolithic, one kind of human — the Cro-Magnon, or *Homo sapiens*[15] — multiplied and fanned out around the world, killing, displacing, or absorbing all other variants of man, then entering new worlds that had never felt a human foot.

By 15,000 years ago at the very latest — long before the ice withdraws — humankind is established on every continent except Antarctica. Like the worldwide expansion of Europe, this prehistoric wave of discovery and migration had profound ecological consequences. Soon after man shows up in new lands, the big game starts to go missing. Mammoths and woolly rhinos retreat north, then vanish from Europe and Asia. A giant wombat, other marsupials, and a tortoise as big as a Volkswagen disappear from Australia. Camels, mammoth, giant bison, giant sloth, and the horse die out across the Americas.[16] A bad smell of extinction follows *Homo sapiens* around the world.

Not all experts agree that our ancestors were solely to blame. Our defenders point out that we hunted in Africa, Asia, and Europe for a million years or more without killing everything off; that many of these extinctions coincide with climatic upheavals; that the end of the Ice Age may have come so swiftly that big animals couldn't adapt or migrate. These are good objections, and it would be unwise to rule them out entirely. Yet the evidence against our ancestors is, I think, overwhelming. Undoubtedly, animals were stressed by the melting of the ice, but they had made it through many similar warmings before. It is also true that earlier people — *Homo erectus*, Neanderthals, and early *Homo sapiens* — had hunted big game without hunting it out. But Upper Palaeolithic people were far better equipped and more numerous than their forerunners, and they killed on a much grander scale.[17] Some of their slaughter sites were almost industrial in size: a thousand mammoths at one; more than 100,000 horses at another.[18] "The Neanderthals were surely able and valiant in the chase," wrote the anthropologist William Howells in 1960, "but they left no such massive bone yards as this."[19] And the ecological moral is underlined more recently by Ian Tattersall. "Like us," he says, "the Cro-Magnons must have had a darker side."[20]

In steep terrain, these relentless hunters drove entire herds over cliffs, leaving piles of animals to rot, a practice that continued into historic times at places such as Head-Smashed-In Buffalo Jump, Alberta. Luckily for bison, cliffs are rare on the great plains. But there would be no limit to the white man's guns that reduced both buffalo and Indian to near extinction in a few decades of the nineteenth century. "The humped herds of buffalo," wrote Herman Melville, "not forty years ago, overspread by tens of thousands the prairies of Illinois and Missouri . . . where now the polite broker sells you land at a dollar an inch."[21] Land at a dollar an inch: now *that* is civilization.

Modern hunter-gatherers — Amazonians, Australian Aboriginals, Inuit, Kalahari "bushmen" — are wise
stewards of their ecologies, limiting their own numbers, treading lightly on the land.[22] It is often assumed
that ancient hunters would have been equally wise. But
archaeological evidence does not support this view. Palaeolithic hunting was the mainstream livelihood, done in
the richest environments on a seemingly boundless earth.
Done, we have to infer from the profligate remains, with
the stock-trader's optimism that there would always be
another big killing just over the next hill. In the last and
best-documented mass extinctions — the loss of flightless
birds and other animals from New Zealand and Mada-
gascar — there is no room for doubt that people were to
blame.[23] The Australian biologist Tim Flannery has called
human beings the "future-eaters." Each extermination is
a death of possibility.[24]

So among the things we need to know about ourselves
is that the Upper Palaeolithic period, which may well
have begun in genocide, ended with an all-you-can-kill
wildlife barbecue. The *perfection* of hunting spelled the
end of hunting as a way of life. Easy meat meant more
babies. More babies meant more hunters. More hunters,
sooner or later, meant less game. Most of the great human
migrations across the world at this time must have been
driven by want, as we bankrupted the land with our
moveable feasts.

The archaeology of western Europe during the final
millennia of the Palaeolithic shows the grand lifestyle of
the Cro-Magnons falling away. Their cave painting falters

and stops. Sculptures and carvings become rare. The flint blades grow smaller, and smaller. Instead of killing mammoth they are shooting rabbits.

In a 1930s essay called "In Praise of Clumsy People," the waggish Czech writer Karel Čapek observed: "Man ceased to be a mere hunter when individuals were born who were very bad hunters." As someone once said of Wagner's music, Čapek's remark is better than it sounds. The hunters at the end of the Old Stone Age were certainly not clumsy, but they were bad because they broke rule one for any prudent parasite: *Don't kill off your host.* As they drove species after species to extinction, they walked into the first progress trap.

Some of their descendants — the hunter-gatherer societies that have survived into recent times — would learn in the school of hard knocks to restrain themselves. But the rest of us found a new way to raise the stakes: that great change known to hindsight as the Farming or Neolithic "Revolution."

Among hunters there had always been a large number of non-hunters: the gatherers — mainly women and children, we suppose, responsible for the wild fruits and vegetables in the diet of a well-run cave. Their contribution to the food supply became more and more important as the game died out.

The people of that short, sharp period known as the Mesolithic, or Middle Stone Age, tried everything: living in estuaries and bogs; beachcombing; grubbing up roots; and reaping wild grasses for the tiny seeds, a practice with enormous implications. So rich were some of these grasses, and so labour-intensive their exploitation, that settled villages appear in key areas *before* farming.[25] Gatherers began to notice that seeds accidentally scattered or passed in droppings would spring up the following year. They began to influence the outcome by tending and enlarging wild stands, sowing the most easily reaped and plumpest seeds.

Such experiments would eventually lead to full agriculture and almost total dependence on a few monotonous staples, but that was several thousand years away; at this early time, the plant-tenders were still mainly gatherers, exploiting a great variety of flora, as well as any wild game and fish they could find. At Monte Verde in Chile, for example, a permanent village of rectangular wooden huts was in place by 13,000 years ago, sustained by hunting camelids, small game, and soon-to-be-extinct mastodon; but the remains include many wild vegetables, not least potato peelings.[26] Although Monte Verde is one of the earliest human sites anywhere in the Americas, it shows a mature and intimate knowledge of local plants, several of which would eventually become the founding crops of Andean civilization.

Like the accumulation of small changes that separated us from the other great apes, the Farming Revolution was an unconscious experiment, too gradual for its initiators to be aware of it, let alone to foresee where it would lead. But compared with all earlier developments, it happened at breakneck speed.

Highly important, for what it tells us about ourselves, is that there was not one revolution but many. On every continent except Australia, farming experiments began soon after the regime of the ice released its grip.[27] Older books (and some recent ones[28]) emphasize the importance of the Middle East, or the Fertile Crescent, which in those days stretched from the Mediterranean shore to the Anatolian plateau and the alluvial plains of Iraq. All the bread-based civilizations derive their staples from this area, which gave us wheat, barley, sheep, and goats.

It is now clear that the Middle East was only one of at least four major regions of the world where agriculture developed independently at about the same time. The others are the Far East, where rice and millet became the main staples; Mesoamerica (Mexico and neighbouring parts of Central America), whose civilizations were based on maize, beans, squash, amaranth, and tomatoes; and the Andean region of South America, which developed many kinds of potato, other tubers, squash, cotton, peanuts, and high-protein grains such as quinoa.[29] In all these heartlands, crop domestication appears between 8,000 and 10,000 years ago.[30] Besides these Big Four, there are about a dozen lesser founding areas around the world, including tropical Southeast Asia, Ethiopia, the Amazon, and eastern North America, which gave us, respectively, the banana, coffee, manioc, and the sunflower.[31] Unconnected peoples sometimes developed the same plants: cotton and peanuts are each of two kinds, developed simultaneously in the New World and the Old.

Animal domestication is harder to document, but at about the same time people were developing crops, they learned that certain herbivores and birds could be followed, corralled, and killed at a sustainable rate. Over generations these animals grew tame enough, and dimwitted enough, not to mind the two-legged serial killer who followed them around. Hunting became herding, just as gathering grew into gardening.

Sheep and goats were the first true domesticates in the Middle East, starting about 8000 B.C. Domestic camelids — early forms of the llama and alpaca, used for pack trains and wool, as well as for meat — appear in Peru during the sixth millennium B.C., about the same time as cattle in Eurasia, though neither camelids nor early cattle were milked. Donkeys and horses were tamed by about 4000 B.C. Craftier creatures such as dogs, pigs, and cats had long been willing to hang around human settlements in return for scraps, slops, and the mouse boom spurred by granaries. Dogs, which may have been tamed for hunting back in the Palaeolithic, are found with human groups throughout the world. In cold weather, they were sometimes used as bedwarmers. In places such as Korea and Mexico, special breeds were kept for meat. The chicken began its sad march towards the maw of Colonel Sanders as a gorgeously feathered Asian jungle fowl, while Mexico domesticated the turkey. Along with the llama and alpaca, Peruvians kept muscovy ducks and the lowly but prolific guinea pig — which even made a cameo appearance on the menu of Christ's Last Supper in a colonial painting.[32]

As the eating of guinea pigs and chihuahuas suggests, the Americas were less well-endowed with domesticable animals than the Old World. But the New World compensated by developing a wider and more productive range of plants. Peru alone had nearly forty major species.[33] Such plants eventually supported huge native cities in the Americas, and several of them would transform the Old World's nutrition and economics when they were introduced there — a matter I shall discuss in the final chapter.

The more predictable the food supply, the bigger the population. Unlike mobile foragers, sedentary people had little reason to limit the number of children, who were useful for field and household tasks. The reproductive rate of women tended to rise, owing to higher levels of body fat and earlier weaning with animal milk and cereal baby food. Farmers soon outnumbered hunter-gatherers — absorbing, killing, or driving them into the surrounding "wilderness."

At the beginning of the Upper Palaeolithic, when our modern subspecies emerged by fair means or foul as the earth's inheritors, we numbered perhaps a third of a million all told.[34] By 10,000 years ago, on the eve of agriculture and after settling all habitable continents, we had increased to about 3 million; and by 5,000 years ago, when farming was established in all the founding regions and full civilization had begun in Sumer and Egypt, we may have reached between 15 and 20 million worldwide.

Such figures are merely educated guesswork, and everything else I have just said is, of course, an oversimplification. The change to full-time farming took millennia, and early results were not always promising, even in a core zone such as the Middle East. Neolithic Jericho was tiny, a mere four acres[35] in 8000 B.C., and it took another 1,500 years to reach ten acres.[36] The Turkish site of Çatal Hüyük, the largest settlement in the Fertile Crescent between 7000 and 5500 B.C., covered only one twentieth of a square mile (or thirty-two acres),[37] and its inhabitants depended on wild game for much of their protein. As any rural Canadian knows, hunting continues among farmers wherever it's fun or worthwhile, and this was especially true in the Americas and parts of Asia where domestic animals were scarce. Nevertheless, the pace of growth accelerated. By about 5,000 years ago, the majority of human beings had made the transition from wild food to tame.

In the magnitude of its consequences, no other invention rivals farming (except, since 1940, the invention of weapons that can kill us all). The human career divides in two: everything before the Neolithic Revolution and everything after it. Although the three Stone Ages — Old, Middle, and New — may seem to belong in a set, they do not. The New Stone Age has much more in common with later ages than with the millions of years of stone toolery that went before it. The Farming Revolution produced an entirely new mode of subsistence, which remains the basis of the world economy to this day. The food technology of the late Stone Age is the one technology we can't live without. The crops of about a dozen ancient peoples feed the 6 billion on earth today. Despite more than two centuries of scientific crop-breeding, the so-called green revolution of the 1960s, and the genetic engineering of the 1990s, not one new staple has been added to our repertoire of crops since prehistoric times.

Although the New Stone Age eventually gave rise to metalworking in several parts of the world, and to the Industrial Revolution in Europe, these were elaborations on the same theme, not a fundamental shift in subsistence. A Neolithic village was much like a Bronze or Iron Age village — or a modern Third World village, for that matter.

The Victorian archaeological scheme of classifying stages of human development by tool materials becomes unhelpful from the Neolithic onward. It may have some merit in Europe, where technology was often linked to social change, but is little help for understanding what happened in places where a lack of the things our technocentric culture regards as basic — metal, ploughs, wheels, etc. — was ingeniously circumvented, or where, conversely, their presence was inconsequential.[38] For example, Mesopotamia invented the wheel about 4000 B.C., but its close neighbour Egypt made no use of wheels for another 2,000 years. The Classic Period Maya, a literate civilization rivalling classical Europe in mathematics and astronomy, made so little use of metals that they were technically in the Stone Age.[39] By contrast, sub-Saharan Africa mastered ironworking by 500 B.C. (as early as China did), yet never developed a full-blown civilization.[40] The Incas of Peru, where metalworking had begun about 1500 B.C., created one of the world's largest and most closely administered empires, yet may have done so without writing as we know it (though evidence is growing that their quipu system was indeed a form of script).[41] Japan made pottery long before anyone else — more than 12,000 years ago — but rice farming and full civilization did not appear there for another 10,000 years, adopted wholesale from China and Korea. The Japanese didn't begin to work bronze until 500 B.C., but became famous for steel swords by the sixteenth century. At that time they acquired European firearms, then abandoned them for 300 years.

We should therefore be wary of technological determinism, for it tends to underestimate cultural factors and reduce complex questions of human adaptation to a simplistic "We're the winners of history, so why didn't others do what we did?" We call agriculture and civilization "inventions" or "experiments" because that is how they look to hindsight. But they began accidentally, a series of seductive steps down a path leading, for most people, to lives of monotony and toil. Farming achieved quantity at the expense of quality: more food and more people, but seldom better nourishment or better lives. People gave up a broad array of wild foods for a handful of starchy roots and grasses — wheat, barley, rice, potatoes, maize. As we domesticated plants, the plants domesticated us. Without us, they die; and without them, so do we. There is no escape from agriculture except into mass starvation, and it has often led there anyway, with drought and blight. Most people, throughout most of time, have lived on the edge of hunger   and much of the world still does.[42]

* * *

In hunter-gatherer societies (barring a few special cases) the social structure was more or less egalitarian, with only slight differences in wealth and power between greatest and least. Leadership was either diffuse, a matter of consensus, or something earned by merit and example. The successful hunter did not sit down beside his kill and stuff himself on the spot; he shared the meat and thereby gained prestige. If a leader became overbearing, or a minority disliked a majority decision, people could leave. In an uncrowded world without fixed borders or belongings, it was easy to vote with one's feet.

The early towns and villages that sprang up in a dozen farming heartlands around the world after the last ice age seem to have continued these free-and-easy ways for a while. Most of them were small peasant communities in which everyone worked at similar tasks and had a comparable standard of living.[43] Land was either communally owned or thought of as having no owner but the gods. Farmers whose effort and skill made them wealthier had an obligation to share with the needy, to whom they were bound by kinship.

Gradually, however, differences in wealth and power became entrenched. Freedom and social opportunity declined as populations rose and boundaries hardened between groups. This pattern first appears in the Neolithic villages of the Middle East, and it has recurred all over the world. The first farmers along the Danube, for example, left only tools in their remains; later settlements are heavily fortified and strewn with weapons. Here, said the great Australian archaeologist Gordon Childe, "we almost see the state of war of all against all arising as . . . land became scarce."[44] Writing those words in 1942, during Hitler's expansionist policy of *Lebensraum*,[45] Childe did not need to underline how little the world had changed from Stone Age times to his.

Patriotism may indeed be, as Dr. Johnson said, "the last refuge of a scoundrel," but it's also the tyrant's first resort. People afraid of outsiders are easily manipulated. The warrior caste, supposedly society's protectors, often become protection racketeers. In times of war or crisis, power is easily stolen from the many by the few on a promise of security. The more elusive or imaginary the foe, the better for manufacturing consent. The Inquisition did a roaring trade against the Devil.[46] And the twentieth century's struggle between capitalism and communism had all the hallmarks of the old religious wars. Was defending either system *really* worth the risk of blowing up the world?

Now we are losing hard-won freedoms on the pretext of a worldwide "war on terror," as if terrorism were something new. (Those who think it is should read *The Secret Agent*, a novel in which anarchist suicide bombers prowl London wearing explosives; it was written by Joseph Conrad a hundred years ago.[47]) The Muslim fanatic is proving a worthy replacement for the heretic, the anarchist, and especially the Red Menace so helpful to military budgets throughout the Cold War.

The Neolithic Revolution seems to have been inevitable, or nearly so, wherever the makings for it were found. If the discovery of farming had been sparked by a freak combination of circumstances, we would expect to see it happen only in one particular place and spread outward from there; or to see it happen very rarely and at widely differing times. Until the Upper Palaeolithic (or shortly before[48]), nature had kept all the meddlesome apes in one big laboratory, the Old World. But once the apes got out and made their way to the New World, there were two laboratories, each stocked with different raw materials and largely cut off from the other when sea levels rose with the melting of the ice.[49] Given that the plants, animals, environments, and technologies in each lab were so different, the astonishing thing is what similar paths were taken on each side of the earth — and how alike the results turned out to be.

When the Spaniards reached the American mainland in the early sixteenth century, the peoples of the western and eastern hemispheres had not met since their ancestors parted as Ice Age hunters running out of game. It is true that there had been a few pre-Columbian contacts — with Polynesians, Vikings, and possibly Asians — but these were too fleeting and too late to affect native flora and fauna or the rise of civilization. Not even such able seamen as the Norway rat and the cockroach had reached America before Columbus. Neither had the Old World's terrible plagues, such as smallpox.[50]

What took place in the early 1500s was truly exceptional, something that had never happened before and never will again. Two cultural experiments, running in isolation for 15,000 years or more, at last came face to face. Amazingly, after all that time, each could recognize the other's institutions. When Cortés landed in Mexico he found roads, canals, cities, palaces, schools, law courts, markets, irrigation works, kings, priests, temples, peasants, artisans, armies, astronomers, merchants, sports, theatre, art, music, and books. High civilization, differing in detail but alike in essentials, had evolved independently on both sides of the earth.

The test case of America suggests that we are predictable creatures, driven everywhere by similar needs, lusts, hopes, and follies. Smaller experiments running independently elsewhere had not reached the same level of complexity, but many showed the same trends. Even on remote Polynesian islands, settled by people descended from a boatload or two of intrepid seafarers, mini-civilizations sprang up complete with social rank, intensive farming, and stone monuments.

Faced not only with the similarity but also the synchronicity of these discrete developments, we have to ask: Why were no crops domesticated anywhere *before* the end of the last ice age? The people of 20,000 years ago were just as smart as those of 10,000 years ago; not all of them were glutted with game, and the ice did not hold sway in lower latitudes.

One possible answer to this question is a worry to us now. By studying ancient ice cores, which, like tree rings, leave a yearly record, climatologists have been able to track the average global temperature over a quarter million years. These studies show that the world's climate has been unusually stable for the past 10,000 years — exactly the lifetime of agriculture and civilization. It seems we couldn't have developed farming earlier, even if we'd tried. The studies also show that the earth's climate has sometimes fluctuated wildly, breaking from an ice age — or plunging into one — not over centuries but in *decades*.[51]

The natural triggers of such events are not well understood. Some sort of chain reaction may provoke the rapid upsets — perhaps a sudden reversal of oceanic currents, or a release of methane from thawing permafrost. In his book on the glacial core studies, Richard Alley points out what should be obvious: "humans have built a civilization adapted to the climate we have. Increasingly, humanity is using everything this climate provides . . . [and] the climate of the last few thousand years is about as good as it gets."[52]

Change is not in our interest. Our only rational policy is not to risk provoking it. Yet we face abundant evidence that civilization itself, through fossil-fuel emissions and other disturbances, is upsetting the long calm in which it grew. Ice sheets at both poles are breaking up. Glaciers in the Andes and Himalayas are thawing; some have disappeared in only twenty-five years.[53] Droughts and unusually hot weather have already caused world grain output to fall or stagnate for eight years in a row. During the same eight years, the number of mouths to feed went up by 600 million.

Steady warming will be bad enough, but the worst outcome would be a sudden overturning of earth's climatic balance — back to its old regime of sweats and chills. If that happens, crops will fail everywhere and the great experiment of civilization will come to a catastrophic end. In the matter of our food, we have grown as specialized, and therefore as vulnerable, as a sabre-toothed cat.

III

FOOLS' PARADISE

THE GREATEST WONDER of the ancient world is how recent it all is. No city or monument is much more than 5,000 years old. Only about seventy lifetimes, of seventy years, have been lived end to end since civilization began.[1] Its entire run occupies a mere 0.2 per cent of the two and a half million years since our first ancestor sharpened a stone.

In the last chapter, I outlined the rise and fall of "man the hunter" in the Old Stone Age. His very progress, his perfection of weapons and techniques, led directly to the end of hunting as a way of life (except in a few places where conditions favoured the prey). Next came the discovery of farming — likely by women — during the New Stone Age, or Neolithic period, in several parts of the world. And from that grew our experiment of civilization, which began as many independent enterprises but, in the past few centuries, has coalesced (mainly by hostile takeover) into one big system that covers and consumes the earth.

There are signs that this experiment, like hunting, is now in danger of falling victim to its own success. I've already mentioned nuclear weapons and greenhouse gases. The big bang in the atom is obviously deadlier than the small bangs in millions of engines; but if we are unlucky or unwise, both could end civilization on its present scale. Much simpler technologies have proved fatal in the past. Sometimes the trouble lies in a particular invention or idea; but it also lies in social structure, in the way people tend to behave when squeezed together in urban civilizations, where power and wealth rise upward and the many are ruled by the few.

In this chapter I want to talk about two traps sprung by progress: one on a small Pacific island, the other on the plains of Iraq.

As I mentioned earlier, the wrecks of our failed experiments lie in deserts and jungles like fallen airliners whose flight recorders can tell us what went wrong. Archaeology is perhaps the best tool we have for looking ahead, because it provides a deep reading of the direction and momentum of our course through time: what we are, where we have come from, and therefore where we are most likely to be going.

Unlike written history, which is often highly edited, archaeology can uncover the deeds we have forgotten, or have chosen to forget. A realistic understanding of the past is quite a new thing, a late fruit of the Enlightenment, although people of many times have felt the tug of what the Elizabethan antiquarian William Camden called the "back-looking curiousity." Antiquity, he wrote, "hath a certaine resemblance with eternity. [It] is a sweet food of the mind."[2]

Not everyone's mind was so open in his day. A Spanish viceroy of Peru who had just seen the Inca capital high in the Andes, with its walls of giant stones fitted like gems, wrote back to his king: "I have examined the fortress that [the Incas] built . . . which shows clearly the work of the Devil . . . for it does not seem possible that the strength and skill of men could have made it."[3]

Even today, some opt for the comforts of mystification, preferring to believe that the wonders of the ancient world were built by Atlanteans, gods, or space travellers, instead of by thousands toiling in the sun. Such thinking robs our forerunners of their due, and us of their experience. Because then one can believe whatever one likes about the past — without having to confront the bones, potsherds, and inscriptions which tell us that people all over the world, time and again, have made similar advances and mistakes.

About two centuries after the Spanish invasion of Peru, a Dutch fleet in the South Seas, far to the west of Chile and below the Tropic of Capricorn, came upon a sight hardly less awesome, and even more inexplicable, than the megalithic buildings of the Andes. On Easter Day, 1722, the Dutchmen sighted an unknown island so treeless and eroded that they mistook its barren hills for dunes.

They were amazed, as they drew near, to see hundreds of stone images, some as tall as an Amsterdam house. "We could not comprehend how it was possible that these people, who are devoid of heavy thick timber [or] strong ropes, nevertheless had been able to erect such images, which were fully thirty feet high."[4] Captain Cook later confirmed the island's desolation, finding "no wood for fuel; nor any fresh water worth taking on board." He described the islanders' tiny canoes, made from scraps of driftwood stitched together like shoe leather, as the worst in the Pacific. Nature, he concluded, had "been exceedingly sparing of her favours to this spot."[5]

The great mystery of Easter Island that struck all early visitors was not just that these colossal statues stood in such a tiny and remote corner of the world, but that the stones seemed to have been put there without tackle, as if set down from the sky. The Spaniards who had credited the Devil with the splendours of Inca architecture were merely unable to recognize another culture's achievements. But even scientific observers could not, at first, account for the megaliths of Easter Island. The figures stood there mockingly, defying common sense.

We now know the answer to the riddle, and it is a chilling one. *Pace* Captain Cook, Nature had not been unusually stingy with her favours.[6] Pollen studies of the island's crater lakes have shown that it was once well watered and green, with rich volcanic soil supporting thick woods of the Chilean wine palm,[7] a fine timber that can grow as big as an oak. No natural disaster had changed that: no eruption, drought, or disease. The catastrophe on Easter Island was man.

Rapa Nui, as Polynesians call the place, was settled during the fifth century A.D. by migrants from the Marquesas or the Gambiers who arrived in big catamarans stocked with their usual range of crops and animals: dogs, chickens, edible rats, sugar cane, bananas, sweet potatoes, and mulberry for making bark cloth.[8] (Thor Heyerdahl's theory that the island was peopled from South America has not been supported by recent work, though sporadic contact between Peru and Oceania probably did take place.[9]) Easter Island proved too cold for breadfruit and coconut palms, but it was rich in seafood: fish, seals, porpoises, turtles, and nesting seabirds. Within five or six centuries, the settlers had multiplied to about 10,000 people — a lot for sixty-four square miles.[10] They built villages with good houses on stone footings and cleared all the best land for fields. Socially they split into clans and ranks — nobles, priests, commoners — and there may have been a paramount chief, or "king." Like Polynesians on some other islands, each clan began to honour its ancestry with impressive stone images. These were hewn from the yielding volcanic tuff of a crater and set up on platforms by the shore. As time went on, the statue cult became increasingly rivalrous and extravagant, reaching its apogee during Europe's high Middle Ages, while the Plantagenet kings ruled England.

Each generation of images grew bigger than the last, demanding more timber, rope, and manpower for hauling to the *ahu*, or altars. Trees were cut faster than they could grow, a problem worsened by the settlers' rats, who ate the seeds and saplings. By A.D. 1400, no more tree pollen is found in the annual layers of the crater lakes: the woods had been utterly destroyed by both the largest and the smallest mammal on the island.

We might think that in such a limited place, where, from the height of Terevaka, islanders could survey their whole world at a glance, steps would have been taken to halt the cutting, to protect the saplings, to replant. We might think that as trees became scarce, the erection of statues would have been curtailed, and timber reserved for essential purposes such as boatbuilding and roofing. But that is not what happened. The people who felled the last tree could *see* it was the last, could know with complete certainty that there would never be another. And they felled it anyway.[11] All shade vanished from the land except the hard-edged shadows cast by the petrified ancestors, whom the people loved all the more because they made them feel less alone.

For a generation or so, there was enough old lumber to haul the great stones and still keep a few canoes seaworthy for deep water. But the day came when the last good boat was gone. The people then knew there would be little seafood and — worse — no way of escape. The word for wood, *rakau*, became the dearest in their language. Wars broke out over ancient planks and worm-eaten bits of jetsam. They ate all their dogs and nearly all the nesting birds, and the unbearable stillness of the place deepened with animal silences. There was nothing left now but the *moai*, the stone giants who had devoured the land. And still these promised the return of plenty, if only the people would keep faith and honour them with increase. But how will we take you to the altars? asked the carvers, and the *moai* answered that when the time came, they would walk there on their own. So the sound of hammering still rang from the quarries, and the crater walls came alive with hundreds of new giants, growing even bigger now they had no need of human transport. The tallest ever set on an altar is over thirty feet high[12] and weighs eighty tons; the tallest ever *carved* is sixty-five feet long[13] and more than *two hundred* tons, comparable to the greatest stones worked by the Incas or Egyptians. Except, of course, that it never budged an inch.

By the end there were more than a thousand *moai*, one for every ten islanders in their heyday. But the good days were gone — gone with the good earth, which had been carried away on the endless wind and washed by flash floods into the sea. The people had been seduced by a kind of progress that becomes a mania, an "ideo-logical pathology," as some anthropologists call it. When Europeans arrived in the eighteenth century, the worst was over; they found only one or two living souls per statue, a sorry remnant, "small, lean, timid and miser-able," in Cook's words.[14] Now without roof beams, many people were dwelling in caves; their only buildings were stone henhouses where they guarded this last non-human protein from one another day and night. The Europeans heard tales of how the warrior class had taken power, how the island had convulsed with burning villages, gory battles, and cannibal feasts. The one innovation of this end-period was to turn the use of obsidian (a razor-keen volcanic glass) from toolmaking to weapons.[15] Daggers and spearheads became the commonest artefacts on the island, hoarded in pits like the grenades and assault rifles kept by modern-day survivalists.

Even this was not quite the nadir. Between the Dutch visit of 1722 and Cook's fifty years later, the people again made war on each other and, for the first time, on the ancestors as well. Cook found *moai* toppled from their platforms, cracked and beheaded, the ruins littered with human bone. There is no reliable account of how or why this happened. Perhaps it started as the ultimate atrocity between enemy clans, like European nations bombing cathedrals in the Second World War.[16] Perhaps it began with the shattering of the island's solitude by strangers in floating castles of unimaginable wealth and menace. These possessors of wood were also bringers of death and disease. Scuffles with sailors often ended with natives gunned down on the beach.[17]

We do not know exactly what promises had been made by the demanding *moai* to the people, but it seems likely that the arrival of an outside world might have exposed certain illusions of the statue cult, replacing compulsive belief with equally compulsive disenchantment. Whatever its animus, the destruction on Rapa Nui raged for at least seventy years. Each foreign ship saw fewer upright statues, until not one giant was left standing on its altar.[18] The work of demolition must have been extremely arduous for the few descendants of the builders. Its thoroughness and deliberation speak of something deeper than clan warfare: of a people angry at their reckless fathers, of a revolt against the dead.

The lesson that Rapa Nui holds for our world has not gone unremarked. In the epilogue to their 1992 book, *Easter Island, Earth Island*, the archaeologists Paul Bahn and John Flenley are explicit. The islanders, they write:

> carried out for us the experiment of permitting unre-stricted population growth, profligate use of resources, destruction of the environment and boundless confidence in their religion to take care of the future. The result was an ecological disaster leading to a population crash. . . . Do we have to repeat the experiment on [a] grand scale? . . . Is the human personality always the same as that of the person who felled the last tree?[19]

The last tree. The last mammoth. The last dodo. And soon perhaps the last fish and the last gorilla. On the basis of what police call "form," we are serial killers beyond reason. But has this always been, and must it always be, the case? Are all human systems doomed to stagger along under the mounting weight of their internal logic until it crushes them? As I have proposed, the answers — and, I think, the remedies — lie in the fates of past societies.

Easter Island was an isolated mini-civilization in a constrained environment. How typical is it of civilization in general? In the previous chapter, I offered a technical definition: that civilizations are large, complex societies based on the domestication of plants, animals, and human beings, with towns, cities, governments, social

classes, and specialized professions. Both ancient and
modern are covered by that. But Easter Island doesn't
meet all the criteria. At 10,000 people, it was small; it
lacked cities, and its political structure was at best that of
a chiefdom, not a state. However, it did have classes and
professions (the stone carvers, for one), and its achievements were in a league with those of far bigger cultures.[20]
Its isolation also makes it uniquely important as a micro-
cosm of more complex systems, including this big island
on which we drift through space. Easter Island punched
way above its weight; but it boxed alone, as if in a
looking-glass, and we have been able to replay the moves
by which it knocked itself out.

Some writers, seeing history in terms of weapons and
winners, have over-emphasized the different rates at
which cultures and continents developed. What strikes
me as more surprising — and highly significant for finding out what kind of creature we humans are — is how
little time it took people to do very similar things independently all around the world, even though they were
working within different cultures and ecologies.

By 3,000 years ago, civilization had arisen in at least
seven places: Mesopotamia, Egypt, the Mediterranean,
India, China, Mexico, and Peru.[21] Archaeology shows that
only about half of these had received their crops and cultural stimuli from others.[22] The rest had built themselves
up from scratch without suspecting that anyone else in
the world was doing the same. This compelling paral-
lelism of ideas, processes, and forms tells us something

important: that given certain broad conditions, human societies everywhere will move towards greater size, complexity, and environmental demand.

Easter Island's little civilization was one of the last to develop independently. The earliest of all was Sumer, in what is now southern Iraq. The Sumerians, whose own ethnic and linguistic stock is unclear, set a pattern that Semitic cultures and others in the Old World would follow.[23] They came to exemplify both the best and worst of the civilized life, and they told us about themselves in cuneiform script on clay tablets, one of the most enduring mediums for the human voice, a writing like the tracks of trained birds. They set down the oldest written stories in the world, a body of texts known as *The Epic of Gilgamesh*, compiled in "strong-walled Uruk, the city of great streets" around the time that Stonehenge and the first Egyptian pyramids were being built. Legends we know from the Hebrew Bible — the Garden of Eden, the Flood — appear in *Gilgamesh* in earlier forms, along with other tales deemed too racy, perhaps, for inclusion in the Pentateuch. One of these, the story of the wild-man Enkidu, who is seduced into the city by "a harlot, a child of pleasure," recalls our transition from the hunting to the urban life:

> And now the wild creatures had all fled away; Enkidu was grown weak, for wisdom was in him, and the thoughts of a man were in his heart. So he returned and sat down at the woman's feet, and listened intently to what she said. "You are wise, Enkidu, and now you have become like a god.

Why do you want to run wild with the beasts in the hills? Come with me. I will take you to strong-walled Uruk, to the blessed temple of Ishtar and of Anu, of love and heaven: there lives [King] Gilgamesh, who is very strong [and who] lords it over men."[24]

In the last chapter, we left the Middle East soon after farming began in the lands often called the Fertile Crescent. Throughout human time this has been the cross-roads of Africa, Europe, and Asia. Back in the Old Stone Age, Neanderthals and Cro-Magnons had contested this turf for 50,000 years — moving north and south with fluctuations in the climate, living at different times in the same rockshelters, possibly evicting one another. I suspect that if we could tune into the Middle Eastern news at almost any period in prehistory, we would find the place seething with creativity and strife, as it has since history began.

But it's a mistake to assume that the Fertile Crescent, for all its natural endowments, its plants and animals suitable for domestication, developed quickly or easily. Even after several thousand years of farming and herding, the biggest Middle Eastern settlements — Jericho (near the Dead Sea) and Çatal Hüyük (in Anatolia) — were still tiny, covering only ten acres and thirty acres, respectively.[25]

Insofar as the Garden of Eden had a physical geography, this was it. The serpent, however, was not the only enemy. Fortifications at Jericho and elsewhere speak of competition for land and a heavier human presence than

the sites alone attest. Nor was the farming life easier or healthier than the hunting life had been: people were smaller in build and worked longer hours than non-farmers. Average life expectancy, deduced from burials at Çatal Hüyük, was twenty-nine years for women and thirty-four for men.[26] By 6000 B.C., there is evidence of widespread deforestation and erosion. Cavalier fire-setting and overgrazing by goats may have been chief culprits, but lime-burning for plaster and whitewash also destroyed the woodland, until it became the thorny scrub and semi-desert seen there today. By 5500 B.C., many of the early Neolithic sites were abandoned.[27] As on Easter Island, people had befouled their nest, or rather had stripped it bare. But unlike the Easter Islanders, these people had room to flee and start again.

Self-driven from Eden (God's flaming sword being perhaps a glint of the fires they had set in the hills), they found a second paradise lower down on the great floodplain of the Tigris and Euphrates, the land called Mesopotamia, or Iraq. The look of this place is fresh in our minds from modern wars: treeless plains and dying oases, salt pans, dust storms, oil slicks, and burnt-out tanks. Here and there, crumbling in the ruthless sun and wind, are great mounds of mud brick — ruins of ancient cities whose names still echo in the cellars of our culture — Babylon, Uruk, and Ur of the Chaldees, where Abraham was born.

Back in the fifth and fourth millennia B.C., southern Iraq had been a marshy delta of channels teeming with fish, reeds taller than a house, and sandbars rich in date palms. Wild boar and waterfowl lived in the canebrakes. The alluvial earth, if tilled, could yield a hundredfold on every seed, for this was new land, laid down at the head of the Persian Gulf. "New" in a manner of speaking: the people who settled here had in effect followed their old fields, which had been washed from the worn hills by the great rivers flowing, as the Bible says, out of Eden.[28]

God had spread a second chance before the children of Adam and Eve, but in this recycled Eden, unlike the first, they would eat only by sweat and toil. "The exploitation of this natural paradise," wrote Gordon Childe in his classic work, *The Most Ancient East*, "required intensive labour and the organized co-operation of large bodies of men. Arable land had literally to be created . . . by a 'separation' of land from water; the swamps must be drained; the floods controlled; the life-giving waters led to the rainless desert by artificial canals."[29] It seems that in this case at least, the hierarchies of civilization grew with the demands of water control.[30]

The scattered mud villages grew into towns. And by 3000 B.C., these towns had become small cities, rebuilt again and again on their own debris until they rose above the plain in earthen mounds known as tells. Throughout most of its thousand-year run, Sumerian civilization was dominated by a dozen such cities, each the heart of a small state. Only twice was a unified kingdom briefly forged: first by the Semitic invader Sargon, and later by the Third Dynasty of Ur. It is thought that four-fifths of the Sumerian population lived in urban centres, and that the entire population was only half a million. (Contemporary Egypt's population was more rural and about three times this size.)[31]

In the early days, Sumerian land was owned communally, and people brought their crops, or at least their surplus, to the city shrine, where a priesthood looked after human and divine affairs — watching the stars, directing irrigation works, improving the crops, brewing and winemaking, and building ever-grander temples. As time went by, the cities grew layer by layer into man-made hills crowned with the typical Mesopotamian step-pyramid, or ziggurat, a sacred mountain commanding the human realm.[32] Such were the buildings the Israelites later lampooned as the Tower of Babel. The priesthoods, which had started as village co-operatives, also grew vertically to become the first corporations, complete with officials and employees, undertaking "the not unprofitable task of administering the gods' estates."[33]

The plains of southern Iraq were rich farmland but lacked most other things town life required. Timber, flint, obsidian, metals, and every block of stone for building, carving, and food-grinding had to be imported, in return for grain and cloth. So wheeled carts, yoked oxen, and use of copper and bronze developed early.[34] Trade and property became highly important, and have been close to the heart of Western culture ever since. Middle Easterners took a mercenary view of their gods as big landowners and themselves as serfs, "toiling in the Lord's vineyard." Unlike the writing of Egypt, China, or Mesoamerica, Sumer's writing was invented not for

sacred texts, divination, literature, or even kingly propaganda, but for accounting.

Over time, the priestly corporations grew bloated and
exploitive, concerned more with their own good than
that of their lowlier members. Though they developed
elements of capitalism, such as private ownership, there
was no free competition of the kind Adam Smith recommended. The Sumerian corporations were monopolies
legitimized by heaven, somewhat like mediaeval monas-
teries or the fiefdoms of televangelists. Their way of life,
however, was far from monastic, as the temple harlotry in
Gilgamesh implies.[35] The Sumerian priests may have been
sincere believers in their gods, though ancient people
were not exempt from manipulations of credulity; at their
worst, they were the world's first racketeers, running the
eternal money-spinners — protection, booze, and girls.[36]

The protection initially offered by the priesthood was
from the forces of nature and the wrath of the gods. But
as the Sumerian city-states grew, they began to make war
among themselves. Their wealth also drew raids from
mountain and desert folk, who, though less civilized,
were often better armed. So it was that Uruk — at 1,100
acres[37] and 50,000 people by far the biggest Sumerian
city[38] — became "strong-walled," the wonder of its world.

"Climb upon the wall of Uruk," invites *Gilgamesh*;
"walk along it, I say; regard the foundation terrace and
examine the masonry: is it not burnt brick and good?"[39]

Having invented irrigation, the city, the corporation,
and writing, Sumer added professional soldiers and
hereditary kings. The kings moved out of the temples

and into palaces of their own,[40] where they forged personal links with divinity, claiming godly status by virtue of descent from heaven, a notion that would appear in many cultures and endure into modern times as divine right.[41] With kingship came new uses for writing: dynastic history and propaganda, the exaltation of a single individual. As Bertolt Brecht dryly reflected in his poem about a worker looking at the Pyramids:

> The books are filled with names of kings.
> Was it kings who hauled the craggy blocks of stone? . . .
> Young Alexander conquered India.
> He alone?

By 2500 B.C., the days of collective landholding by city and corporation were gone; the fields now belonged to lords and great families. The Sumerian populace became serfs and sharecroppers,[42] and beneath them was a permanent underclass of slaves — a feature of Western civilization that would last until the nineteenth century after Christ.

States arrogate to themselves the power of coercive violence: the right to crack the whip, execute prisoners, send young men to the battlefield. From this stems that venomous bloom which J. M. Coetzee has called, in his extraordinary novel *Waiting for the Barbarians*, "the black flower of civilization"[43] — torture, wrongful imprisonment, violence for display — the forging of might into right.

Among the privileges of god-kings in Sumer and elsewhere were various styles of human sacrifice, including the right to take people along for company beyond the grave. The King's Tomb at Ur, known to archaeologists as the Death Pit, contains the first mass burial of royal concubines, retainers, and the workers who built it — about seventy-five men and women all told, their skeletons nested like spoons in a drawer.[44] Around the world, from Egypt and Greece to China and Mexico, the idea that the king's life was worth so much more than other people's would take root again and again.[45] The builders who seal the tomb are killed on the spot by guards, who are themselves killed by other guards, and so on, until the late king's executors deem his resting place sufficiently honoured and secure.

Since we tend to regard ancient North America as non-urban and libertarian, one of the most surprising instances of servant burial comes from Cahokia — a pre-Columbian city about the same size as Uruk — whose earthen pyramids still stand beside the Mississippi, near St. Louis.[46]

Throughout the ancient world, rulers performed the ultimate political theatre: public sacrifice of captives. As a nineteenth-century Ashanti king candidly told the British: "If I were to abolish human sacrifice, I should deprive myself of one of the most effectual means of keeping the people in subjection."[47] The British, who at that time were tying Indian mutineers across the mouths of cannon and blowing them in half, scarcely needed such advice. Each culture has its codes and sensibilities. In Mexico, the Spanish conquistadores were appalled by the ritual slaughter of prisoners, done with a blade to the heart. The Aztecs were equally horrified when they saw the Spaniards burn people alive.

Violence is as old as man, but civilizations commit it with a deliberation that lends it special horror. In the Death Pit of Ur we can foreglimpse all the mass graves to come, down through 5,000 years to Bosnia and Rwanda and full circle to the Iraq of Saddam Hussein, who, like the ancient kings of that land, had his name stamped on the bricks used to rebuild their monuments. In civilization, unlike the hunter-gatherer life, it has always mattered who you are. We have come a very long way from extended families around an Old Stone Age campfire to societies in which some people are demigods and others nothing more than flesh to be worked to death or buried in their betters' tombs.[48]

Until mechanized farming began, food growers, whether peasants or slaves, outnumbered the elite and professionals who lived off their surplus by about ten to one. The masses' reward for this was usually little more than bare survival, alleviated by the consolations of custom and belief. If they were lucky, they belonged to a state that, in enlightened self-interest, would give public assistance in times of crop failure. The ideal of the leader as provider, and the wealthy as open-handed, survived to some extent and can be traced in many languages. Our word "lord" comes from the Old English *hlaford*, or "loaf-ward," he who guarded the bread supply — and was expected to share it. The Inca title *qhapaq* meant "munificent," someone who gathers wealth in but also redistributes it. Another title of the Inca emperor was *wakchakuyaq*, "he who cares for the bereft."[49] The chiefs of Hawaii were warned by their elders against hoarding food or goods: "The hands of the Arii must always be open; on [this] rests your prestige."[50] And it was said of the Chinese emperors that their first duty was to feed their people. The truth is that China, like most agrarian societies, lurched from famine to famine well into modern times.[51] Effective food security was as rare in the past as it is today in the Third World. Most ancient states did not have the storage capacity or transport to deal with anything worse than a minor crisis. The Incas and Romans were probably the best at famine relief, and it's no coincidence that both were very large empires spread over several climatic zones, with good warehousing, roads, and sea lanes.

A small civilization such as Sumer, dependent on a single ecosystem and without high ground, was especially vulnerable to flood and drought. Such disasters were viewed, then as now, as "acts of God" (or gods). Like us, the Sumerians were only dimly aware that human activity was also to blame. Floodplains will always flood, sooner or later, but deforestation of the great watersheds upstream made inundations much fiercer and more deadly than they would otherwise have been. Woodlands, with their carpet of undergrowth, mosses, and loam, work like great sponges, soaking up rainfall and allowing it to filter slowly into the earth below; trees drink up water and breathe it into the air. But wherever primaeval woods and their soils have been destroyed by cutting, burning, overgrazing, or ploughing, the bare subsoil bakes hard in dry weather and acts like a roof in wet. The result is flash floods, sometimes carrying such heavy loads of silt and gravel that they rush from steep ravines like liquid concrete. Once the waters reach a floodplain, they slow down, dump their gravel, and spread out in a brown tide that oozes its way to the sea.

Staggering alluvial forces are at work in Mesopotamia. In the 5,000 years since Sumerian records began, the twin rivers have filled in eighty miles[52] of the Persian Gulf. Iraq's second city of Basra was open sea in ancient times.[53] The plains of Sumer are more than two hundred miles[54] wide. In times of an unusually great flood — the kind that might happen once a century or so — a king standing in the rain on a temple softening under his feet would see nothing but water between himself and the rim of the sky.

Not only did Adam and Eve drive themselves from Eden, but the eroded landscape they left behind set the stage for Noah's Flood.[55] In the early days, when the city-mounds were low and easily swamped, the only refuge would have been a boat. The Sumerian version of the legend, told in the first person by a man named Utnapishtim, has the ring of real events, with vivid detail on freak weather and broken dams.[56] In it we may see not only the forerunner of the biblical story but the first eyewitness account of a man-made environmental catastrophe:

In those days the world teemed, the people multiplied. . . .
Enlil heard the clamour and he said to the gods in council,

"The uproar of mankind is intolerable and sleep is no longer possible. . . ." So the gods agreed to exterminate mankind.[57]

Enlil, the storm god, is the instigator; others, including Ishtar, goddess of love and queen of heaven (a less virginal forerunner of Mary), go along. But Ea, the god of wisdom, warns Utnapishtim in a dream: "Tear down your house, I say, and build a boat, abandon possessions and look for life. . . . Take up into the boat the seed of all living creatures."

The time was fulfilled, the evening came, the rider of the storm sent down the rain. I looked out at the weather and it was terrible, so I too boarded the boat and battened her down. . . . With the first light of dawn a black cloud came from the horizon; it thundered within where Adad, lord of the storm, was riding. . . . Then the gods of the abyss rose up; Nergal pulled out the dams of the nether waters, Ninurta the warlord threw down the dykes, and . . . the god of the storm turned daylight to darkness, when he smashed the land like a cup. . . .

For six days and nights the winds blew, torrent and tempest and flood overwhelmed the world. . . . When the seventh day dawned . . . I looked at the face of the world and there was silence, all mankind was turned to clay. The surface of the sea stretched as flat as a rooftop; I opened a hatch and the light fell on my face. Then I bowed down low, I sat down and I wept . . . for on every side was the waste of water.

Utnapishtim sends out birds to find land. When the waters start to go down, he burns incense to draw down the gods, but his wording hints that the real attraction is the stench of corpses in the mud: the gods, he says, "gathered like flies over the sacrifice." Unlike Jehovah with his rainbow, the Sumerian deities make no promises. Ishtar fingers her necklace and says only that she will remember. Enlil sees the ark and gets angry: "Has any of these mortals escaped? Not one was to have survived." Then Ea, who had given the warning and saved the animals, upbraids Enlil for what he has done and begins a doleful chant:

> Would that a lion had ravaged mankind
> Rather than the flood. . . .
> Would that famine had wasted the world
> Rather than the flood.

Ea should have been more careful what he wished for. When Sir Leonard Woolley excavated in Sumer between the world wars, he wrote: "To those who have seen the Mesopotamian desert . . . the ancient world seem[s] well-nigh incredible, so complete is the contrast between past and present. . . . Why, if Ur was an empire's capital, if Sumer was once a vast granary, has the population dwindled to nothing, the very soil lost its virtue?"[58]

His question had a one-word answer: salt. Rivers rinse salt from rocks and earth and carry it to the sea. But when people divert water onto arid land, much of it evaporates and the salt stays behind. Irrigation also causes waterlogging, allowing brackish groundwater to seep upward. Unless there is good drainage, long fallowing, and enough rainfall to flush the land, irrigation schemes are future salt pans.

Southern Iraq was one of the most inviting areas to begin irrigation, and one of the hardest in which to sustain it: one of the most seductive traps ever laid by progress. After a few centuries of bumper yields, the land began to turn against its tillers. The first sign of trouble was a decline in wheat, a crop that behaves like the coalminer's canary. As time went by, the Sumerians had to replace wheat with barley, which has a higher tolerance for salt. By 2500 B.C. wheat was only 15 per cent of the crop, and by 2100 B.C. Ur had given up wheat altogether.

As builders of the world's first great watering schemes, the Sumerians can hardly be blamed for failing to foresee their new technology's consequences. But political and cultural pressures certainly made matters worse. When populations were smaller, the cities had been able to sidestep the problem by lengthening fallow periods, abandoning ruined fields, and bringing new land under production, albeit with rising effort and cost. After the mid-third millennium, there was no new land to be had. Population was then at a peak, the ruling class top-heavy, and chronic warfare required the support of standing armies — nearly always a sign, and a cause, of trouble. Like the Easter Islanders, the Sumerians failed to reform their society to reduce its environmental impact.[59] On the contrary, they tried to intensify production, especially during the Akkadian empire (c. 2350–2150 B.C.) and their swan song under the Third Dynasty of Ur, which fell in 2000 B.C.

The short-lived Empire of Ur exhibits the same behaviour as we saw on Easter Island: sticking to entrenched beliefs and practices, robbing the future to pay the present, spending the last reserves of natural capital on a reckless binge of excessive wealth and glory. Canals were lengthened, fallow periods reduced, population increased, and the economic surplus concentrated on Ur itself to support grandiose building projects. The result was a few generations of prosperity (for the rulers), followed by a collapse from which southern Mesopotamia has never recovered.[60]

By 2000 B.C., scribes were reporting that the earth had "turned white."[61] All crops, including barley, were failing. Yields fell to a third of their original levels. The Sumerians' thousand years in the sun of history came to an end. Political power shifted north to Babylon and Assyria, and much later, under Islam, to Baghdad. Northern Mesopotamia is better drained than the south, but even there the same cycle of degradation would be repeated by empire after empire, down to modern times. No one, it seems, was willing to learn from the past. Today, fully half of Iraq's irrigated land is saline — the highest proportion in the world, followed by the other two centres of floodplain civilization, Egypt and Pakistan.[62]

As for the ancient cities of Sumer, a few struggled on as villages, but most were utterly abandoned. Even after 4,000 years, the land around them remains sour and barren, still white with the dust of progress. The desert in which Ur and Uruk stand is a desert of their making.

IV

PYRAMID SCHEMES

IN THE FORESTS OF Yucatán and Belize dwells a lovely but sinister temptress whom the Maya call the Xtabay. She is seen by lone hunters who have spent too long in the bush, and she drives them mad with lust. They glimpse her through the leaves and cannot help but follow, oblivious as the twilight thickens. They go on following, getting so close that they can smell the Xtabay's wild scent and feel the delicious flick of her long hair. When they wake up (*if* they wake up, for many are never seen again), they do so cut and bleeding, with their britches down, completely lost.

Sex, food, wealth, power, prestige: they lure us onward, make us progress. And to these we can add progress itself, in its modern meaning of material things getting better and better, an idea that arose with the Industrial Revolution and became its great article of faith.[1] The two ancient societies whose careers I've outlined so far, Easter Island and Sumer, probably had no such notion of progress, yet they were seduced and ruined by their own desires all the same.

But how typical were they of civilizations as a whole? Is civilization inherently maladaptive, an experiment doomed by its own dynamics? Ruins all over the earth seem to say so. Yet the presence of modern civilization everywhere seems to contradict the past. Is ours the exception that has tamed the Xtabay and will live with her happily ever after?

In this chapter I shall first outline the two most famous cases of internal collapse — the fall of Rome in the fourth century A.D. and of the Classic Maya in the ninth — and then look briefly at two hardy perennials, Egypt and China. The Roman and Maya civilizations were much later, larger, and in the case of Rome at least, far more complex than the Sumerian. Like the Sumerians, the Classic Maya lived in a constellation of rival city-states. But their peak population was about ten times greater, between 5 and 7 million, all told.[2] The Roman Empire, at its height, ruled some 50 million people — a quarter of the human race at the time.

The Maya and Romans had no connection with each other. They arose at similar times but in separate social laboratories: the New World and the Old. This makes them useful for recognizing human behaviours that transcend specifics of time, place, and culture — patterns that I think can help us answer two of Gauguin's questions: *What are we?* and *Where are we going?*

Easter Island and Sumer wrecked their environments so thoroughly, and fell so hard, that they became effectively extinct.[3] But Rome and the Maya managed to linger in simplified "mediaeval" forms after their collapses, leaving direct descendants who are part of today's world. Rome's heirs were the Byzantine Empire and the European nations who speak modern dialects of Latin. The Maya were not empire builders, and any renaissance they might have achieved was forestalled by the Spanish invasion in the sixteenth century. Yet the death of their culture has been exaggerated. Eight million people speak Mayan languages today — roughly the same number as in the Classic Period — and many of them practise distinctly Maya forms of social organization, belief, art, and calendrical astrology.[4]

In my dystopian novel, *A Scientific Romance*, a character calls civilization "a pyramid scheme," and a few years later I used the phrase for the title of an article that became the seed of this book.[5] A pyramid of stone or brick, which may also take the shape of colossal statues, tombs, or office towers, is the outward and visible sign of a human social pyramid. And the human pyramid is in turn carried by a less visible natural pyramid — the food chain and all other resources in the surrounding ecology, often termed "natural capital."

The careers of Rome and the Maya also show, I think, that civilizations often behave like "pyramid" sales schemes, thriving only while they grow. They gather wealth to the centre from an expanding periphery, which may be the frontier of a political and trading empire or a colonization of nature through intensified use of resources, often both.

Such a civilization is therefore most unstable at its peak, when it has reached maximum demand on the ecology. Unless a new source of wealth or energy appears, it has no room left to raise production or absorb the shock of natural fluctuations. The only way onward is to keep wringing new loans from nature and humanity.

Once nature starts to foreclose — with erosion, crop failure, famine, disease — the social contract breaks down. People may suffer stoically for a while, but sooner or later the ruler's relationship with heaven is exposed as a delusion or a lie. Then the temples are looted, the statues thrown down, the barbarians welcomed, and the emperor's naked rump is last seen fleeing through a palace window.

I should make a distinction between true collapses and political upheavals such as the French, Russian, and Mexican revolutions. Although land misuse and hunger were important in these upheavals, their prime cause was the exhaustion of social, not natural, capital. Once these societies reorganized, the business of civilization not only continued but expanded. A true collapse results in a society's extinction or near-extinction, during which very large numbers of people die or scatter. Recovery, if there is one, takes centuries, for it requires the regeneration of natural capital, as woods, water, and topsoil slowly rebuild.

* * *

Picture the world during the heyday of Rome on the eve of the year 180, when Marcus Aurelius died and the long agony of decline began. In the two millennia that had gone by since the fall of Sumer, civilizations had flowered all around the earth. On a typical second-century day, the sun would rise on Han China, pass over the Buddhist stupas of Mauryan India, glare down on the brick ruins of the Indus and Euphrates valleys, and take more than two hours to traverse the Roman lake of the Mediterranean. By the time it was noon at Gibraltar, worshippers would be greeting the dawn from the tops of pyramids in highland Mexico, the Guatemalan jungle, and the irrigated valleys of Peru. Only as the sun moved west across the Pacific would it shine on no cities or stone temples, but even here the planting and building had already begun — from Fiji to the Marquesas, the first Polynesian stepping stones across the ocean hemisphere.

Athens had faded after the fourth century B.C., but not before Alexander had spread Greek culture and colonists from the Dardanelles to northern India. Egypt, the most conservative civilization of all time, had experienced many periods of decay and renewal, but still retained her ancient character behind a European façade along the Nile delta.

In the second century A.D., declared Edward Gibbon in his *Decline and Fall of the Roman Empire*, "the empire of Rome comprehended the fairest part of the earth, and the most civilised portion of mankind."[6] People of non-European descent might dispute those claims, but Gibbon was certainly right when he added that Rome's fall "will ever be remembered, and is still felt by the nations of the earth." The descendants of Rome and the Classic Maya did meet eventually — when the Spaniards invaded the New World. All Europe's empires, and neo-Europes such as the United States,[7] tried to mould themselves on imagined Classical ideals, though the real Rome was hardly the imperium of order and clean marble suggested by its surviving architecture.[8] Like every society, the Romans lurched from crisis to crisis, making the rules as they went along. In truth, English-speaking democracy owes as much to the Anglo-Saxons as it does to a Classical model.

In the last chapter I mentioned that the first farming villages in the world appeared in the uplands of the Fertile Crescent, or the Middle East, and that mankind drove itself from this Eden in the sixth millennium B.C. by denuding the land. Thousands of years later, the sad story was replayed in the Mediterranean basin, especially in hilly terrain once thickly covered by old-growth forests, an ecosystem of which hardly a trace survives today. Once again, the principal villains across Greece, southern Italy, southern France, and Spain were fires, goats, and timber-felling. A herd of goats is not only meat and milk but capital on the hoof, hoarded in good times and sold or eaten when necessary. Able to thrive almost anywhere, goats often create an environment in which little but goats will survive.

Woodlands can withstand a certain level of burning and felling, but if too many grazing animals are present, the seedlings get eaten and the woods die of old age. Wild grazers are thinned out by predators, including humans. But herders often keep so many animals that grazing pressure is relentless.[9] In times of high population and rural poverty, grazing is often followed by the tilling of hillsides — hoes or ploughs delivering the final blow to whatever soil remains, a common sight in the so-called developing world today.[10]

The Athenians became alarmed by deforestation early in the sixth century B.C. Greek city populations were growing quickly at that time, most of the timber was already cut, and the poor were farming goat-stripped hills with disastrous results. Unlike the Sumerians, who may have been unaware of the destruction caused by their irrigation methods until it was too late, the Greeks understood what was happening and tried to do something. In 590 B.C., the statesman Solon, realizing that rural poverty and land alienation by powerful Athenian nobles lay behind much of the trouble, outlawed debt-serfdom and food exports; he also tried to ban farming on steep slopes. A generation later, Pisistratus, another ruler of Athens, offered grants for olive planting, which would have been an effective reclamation measure, especially if combined with terracing.[11] But as with such efforts in our day, funding and political will were unequal to the task. Some 200 years later, in his unfinished dialogue *Critias*, Plato wrote a vivid account of the damage, showing a sophisticated knowledge of the connection between water and woods:

What now remains compared with what then existed is like the skeleton of a sick man, all the fat and soft earth having wasted away. . . . Mountains which now have nothing but food for bees . . . had trees not very long ago. [The land] was enriched by the yearly rains, which were not lost to it, as now, by flowing from the bare land into the sea; but the soil was deep, and therein received the water, and kept it in the loamy earth . . . feeding springs and streams running everywhere. Now only abandoned shrines remain to show where the springs once flowed.[12]

It is no coincidence that Greek power and achievement began to wane about this time. Archaeology reveals a similar picture elsewhere around the Mediterranean. Southern Italy and Sicily were well wooded until about 300 B.C., but the woods quickly shrank as Rome and other cities grew, making heavy demands for timber, charcoal, and meat. Livestock and landholding patterns were again to blame. In several watersheds, so much earth was swept away from hillsides to estuaries that it formed malarial marshes and silted up ports such as Ostia and Paestum. Rome did not collapse for many more centuries, so this early degradation obviously wasn't severe enough to bring down the economy, but it accounts for shrinking agricultural output, growing reliance on imported grain, and rural decline in the heart of Italy. "Long ago," wrote the poet Ovid shortly before the time of Christ,

Earth . . . had better things to offer — crops without
    cultivation,
fruit on the bough, honey in the hollow oak.

> No one tore the ground with ploughshares
> or parcelled out the land
> or swept the sea with dipping oars —
> the shore was the world's end.
> Clever human nature, victim of your inventions,
> disastrously creative,
> why cordon cities with towered walls?
> Why arm for war?[13]

Until the time of Julius Caesar, Rome's conquests were essentially private enterprises. Roman citizens who went to war came back with booty, slaves, and a flow of tribute exacted by local agents on commission whose techniques included extortion and loansharking. Cicero claims that Brutus lent money to a Cypriot town at an interest rate of 48 per cent — evidently a common practice, and an early precedent for Third World debt.[14]

Whether they were well-born patricians or overnight millionaires, Rome's soldiers of fortune wanted to enjoy and display their winnings at home. The result was a land boom everywhere within range of the capital. Peasants were dispossessed and driven onto unsuitable land, with environmental consequences like those that Solon had recognized in Athens. Family farms could not compete against big estates using slave labour; they went bankrupt or were forced to sell out, and their young men joined the legions. The ancient commons of the Roman peasantry were alienated with even less legality. As in Sumer, public land passed quickly into private hands, a situation the Gracchus brothers tried to remedy with land reform in the late second century B.C. But the reform failed, the commons were lost, and the state had to placate the lower orders by handing out free wheat, a solution that became expensive as the urban proletariat increased. By the time of Claudius, 200,000 Roman families were on the dole.[15]

One of the revealing ironies of Rome's history is that the city-state's native democracy withered as its empire grew. Real power passed from the senate into the willing hands of field commanders, such as Julius Caesar, who controlled whole armies and provinces. It must be said that in return for power, Caesar gave Rome intelligent reforms — a precedent often invoked by despots impatient with the law. "Necessity," wrote Milton, is always "the tyrant's plea."[16]

Ancient civilizations were generally of two types — city-state systems or centralized empires — both of which arose independently in the Old and New worlds.[17] With the eclipse of its republic by its empire, Rome changed from the first kind of polity into the second. (A similar evolution has happened in other times and places, but is not by any means inevitable. Several modern countries, including Canada and the United States, show characteristics of both types.)

Some years after Julius Caesar's murder and a further round of civil wars, the senate made a deal with Caesar's great-nephew Octavian, who took the name Augustus and the new office of *princeps*. These measures were supposed to be a special case, for his lifetime only. In theory, he was the chief magistrate and the writ of the republic still ran. In reality, a new age of quasi-monarchy had begun.[18] The empire had outgrown the institutions of its founding city.

Augustus and many of his successors proved able and enlightened rulers. Most of them understood, as he did, that the time for consolidation and integration of the empire had come. A hawkish dream of reconquering Alexander's domains was quietly dropped.[19] The empire's eastern boundary was fixed at the Euphrates and along the Rhine and Danube. The other main borders were natural: the Sahara and Arabian deserts, and the Atlantic shore.

The Augustan order lasted, with various upsets, for nearly two centuries; the western empire would then take another two centuries to die. The capital city continued to grow long after its dominions had begun to fray at the edges; as in modern countries, unrest in the provinces drove people to the centre. Rome may have reached its highest population around the time Constantine split the empire early in the fourth century A.D. Whether it held a million then (as some claim) or about half that, it was still the biggest city on earth, surpassing contemporaries in China and Mexico which had several hundred thousand each.[20]

Cities of millions are a recent phenomenon, dependent on mechanized transport. In the time of Henry VIII, the largest towns in western Europe — Paris, London, Seville — held about 50,000 people each, the same as Uruk in the days of Gilgamesh. When Queen Victoria died, there were only sixteen cities in the world of one million or more; now there are at least 400.[21] All pre-industrial cities were constrained by the difficulty of getting supplies in and wastes out every day, a problem not always eased by horses and carts. The best solution was water transport by a network of canals, as in Venice and Aztec Mexico City.[22]

The unsavoury truth is that until the mid-nineteenth century, most cities were death traps, seething with disease, vermin, and parasites. Average life expectancy in ancient Rome was only nineteen or twenty years — much lower than in Neolithic Çatal Hüyük,[23] but slightly better than in Britain's Black Country, evoked so vividly by Dickens, where the average fell to seventeen or eighteen.[24] Without a constant inflow of soldiers, slaves, merchants, and hopeful migrants, neither ancient Rome nor Georgian London could have kept its numbers up. Rome had several serious pandemics, possibly of Asian origin. While these caused manpower and fiscal problems, they may also have postponed the empire's decline by relieving pressure on the land.

Explanations for Rome's fall run the gamut — plagues, lead poisoning, mad emperors, corruption, barbarians, Christianity — and Joseph Tainter, in his book on social collapses, has added Parkinson's Law. Complex systems, he argues, inevitably succumb to diminishing returns. Even if other things remain equal, the costs of running and defending an empire eventually grow so burdensome that it becomes more efficient to throw off the whole imperial superstructure and revert to local forms of organization. By the time of Constantine, the imperial standing army was more than half a million men, an enormous drain on a treasury whose revenue depended mainly on agriculture, especially as many great landowners had been granted tax exemptions.

The government's solution was to debase the currency used for payrolls; eventually the denarius contained so little silver that it became, in effect, paper money. Inflation of Weimar proportions ensued. A measure of Egyptian wheat that had sold for half a denarius in the empire's heyday cost 10,000 denarii by A.D. 338. At the beginning of the fourth century, it took 4,000 silver coins to buy one gold solidus; by the end of the century, it took 180 million.[25] Citizens worn down by inflation and unfair taxation began defecting to the Goths.[26]

Because Rome was a literate society, we know of such woes as they affected higher levels of the human pyramid. But beneath the ills of the body politic lay a steady degradation of the natural pyramid that sustained the whole enterprise. Archaeological work in Italy and Spain has revealed severe erosion corresponding to high levels of agricultural activity during imperial times, followed by population collapse and abandonment until the late Middle Ages.[27]

As the empire impoverished the soils of southern Europe, Rome exported its environmental load to colonies, becoming dependent on grain from North Africa and the Middle East. The consequences can be seen in those regions today. Antioch, capital of Roman Syria, lies under some thirty feet[28] of silt washed down from deforested hills, and the great Libyan ruins of Leptis Magna now stand in a desert.[29] Rome's ancient breadbaskets are filled with sand and dust.

That is not, of course, the whole story. Rome controlled many environments, not all of which were exploited so destructively. Europe north of the Alps, with its wetter climate and heavy soils unsuited to the crude ploughs of the time, stayed lightly settled. Roman London was only half a square mile,[30] and the spa town of Bath, whose walls impressed an early English poet as "a kingly thing . . . the work of giants,"[31] covered only two dozen acres.[32]

Mediaeval history confirms the archaeological evidence: the empire fell hardest at its core, the Mediterranean basin, where the brunt of the environmental cost was borne. Power then shifted to the periphery, where Germanic invaders such as Goths, Franks, and English founded small ethnic states on northern lands that Rome had not exhausted.

The great city itself was looted and half-abandoned, the prize of endless barbarian and papal wars. Its population would not again reach half a million until the twentieth century.

While Rome was conquering one quarter of humanity, another quarter — that living in the Americas — was, as I've noted, running similar social experiments.[33] During the first millennium B.C., a civilization named Chavín spread its ornate art style across much of Peru.[34] Soon after the time of Christ, the stone temples of Tiwanaku rose beside Lake Titicaca, at an altitude of nearly 13,000 feet,[35] one of the highest cities ever built.[36]

The largest city in the Americas during the Roman Empire's heyday was Teotihuacan in central Mexico, one of few urban centres anywhere that rivalled the scale of Rome at the time. Covering eight square miles,[37] with stepped pyramids flanking a broad ceremonial avenue at the axis of a grid, it was grander in layout than Rome itself, though smaller in population.[38]

Mesoamerican civilization had emerged about 1200 B.C. with the Olmecs of the Mexican gulf; their architecture, sculpture, and mathematics inspired both Teotihuacan and the Maya, a people who have lived in Guatemala, Yucatán, and Honduras for at least 4,000 years.[39] Archaeologists define the Maya Classic Period as beginning about A.D. 200 with the rise of kingship and royal inscriptions, but Maya civilization was established long before that. A glyphic text from 400 B.C. has been found, and some of the biggest Maya temples ever built went up during the second century B.C. at Calakmul and El Mirador.[40] The foundations of one building cover twenty-two acres[41] — a footprint the size of Roman Bath.[42]

Our stock image of the Maya — one that appeared at the end of the first Star Wars film — is of temples rearing like battered skyscrapers from an emerald jungle canopy. That scene was shot at the ruins of Tikal, the foremost Maya city of the Late Classic Period, now a wildlife sanctuary for hundreds of bird species and rare animals such as ocelot and jaguar. Twelve hundred years ago, when those temples were last in daily use, little if any jungle would have been in sight. Like a Sumerian king atop his ziggurat, the lord of Tikal would have gazed out upon a man-made landscape: a dense urban core with half a dozen steep temples two hundred feet[43] high, then palaces and suburbs, then fields and farms stretching to the horizon, where neighbouring cities rose against the sky.

As in other city-state systems, Maya civilization was internally competitive, artistically and intellectually fertile. The pre-Classic Maya (along with the Olmecs) were the first people in the world to develop full positional numerals with the concept of zero. This mathematical idea, which seems so obvious today, was invented only twice in history. It eluded the Greeks and all of Europe until the Arabic system (which developed in India about A.D. 600) ousted cumbersome Roman numerals in the late Middle Ages.[44] Mesoamerica was also one of only three or four places to invent writing, which the Maya developed into a phonetic as well as glyphic system.[45] (The others were Sumer, China, and possibly Egypt; the rest of the world's scripts were either derived from these or stimulated by knowledge of writing's existence in a neighbouring society.[46])

Using their advanced arithmetic in a calendar known as the Long Count, the Maya charted the mystery of time, recording astronomical events and running mythological calculations far into the past and future — sometimes over millions of years.[47] Calendars are power, as Julius Caesar, who named the month of July after himself, was also aware. Only three ancient Maya books have survived, but they are enough to reveal the most accurate astronomy until Europe's Renaissance, by which time Caesar's calendar had drifted ten days out of step with the sun.

The social contract between Maya kings and their subjects was that, through special knowledge and ritual, the rulers would keep earth in tune with heaven, ensuring good harvests and prosperity. They succeeded too well. By the height of the Late Classic Period in the eighth century A.D., rural populations were as dense as those in pre-industrial Southeast Asia.[48] The Tikal kingdom alone may have held half a million people, depending on how its boundaries were defined.[49] The other states — a dozen important ones and perhaps fifty more — were much smaller and seem to have been arranged in shifting alliances, rather like modern nations.

Most Maya lived on the land in farmsteads. Even far from a city, they numbered up to 500 a square mile[50] on good soil.[51] It used to be a mystery how the fragile ecology of a tropical rainforest, believed to have been cultivated by swidden (slash and burn), could support such densities. It is now known that the Maya practised intensive farming in swamps by a method called raised fields, cutting networks of canals and ditches to drain land in the rainy season and water it in the dry. Fish were kept in these canals, whose dredgings were used as fertilizer along with compost and sewage. As Victorians in India coyly put it, Maya fields were "self-manuring."[52]

Maya towns, like most small societies, had been communitarian at first — but a familiar social pyramid rose up with the pyramids of stone. And nature, of course, had to carry it all. Studies of ancient pollen confirm that as the cities grew, the jungle died by the stone axe. Cornfields spread and trees dwindled, with a corresponding decline in game, the Mayas' chief source of protein apart from fish, turkeys, and an occasional hairless dog. By the middle of the Classic Period, only the upper class was eating much meat in the larger states.

Each city had its distinctive style. Copan produced intricate sculpture, the statues of its kings (compared by Aldous Huxley to Chinese ivories) radiating order and refinement.[53] Palenque's palaces were light and imaginative, embellished with bas-relief panels and finely modelled stucco. Tikal became a massive, vertical place, its central buildings the tallest in the Americas until the late nineteenth century — a Manhattan of art deco towers. (The resemblance isn't fanciful: Maya architecture influenced modern styles, especially early skyscraper forms and the work of Frank Lloyd Wright.[54])

Now that Maya inscriptions can be read, they have dispelled old notions of Classic Period life as lofty and serene. For all the grand explorations of cosmic time, public texts are also royal propaganda, proclaiming births, accessions, deaths, victories, and *coups d'etat*. During the eighth century, as trouble begins to brew, these statements become more strident, betraying a scramble for power and resources in a shrinking world. Militarism takes hold, old alliances break down, dynasties become unstable, the ruling class exalts itself with extravagant building projects. Tikal was built up over 1,500 years, but all the high towers that still watch over the forest went up in the city's final century, costly blooms on the eve of collapse.[55]

When the great cities wobbled, upstarts began to assert themselves, as happened in Greece during the

Peloponnesian Wars. At the Maya town of Dos Pilas, which made a futile bid for power in the mid-eighth century, diggings have unearthed a glimpse of the last days — people huddling in the central square, tearing stone from the temples to throw up barricades. Equally poignant are the wall paintings at the small city of Bonampak, which commissioned a set of frescoes to record a great victory in the 790s.[56] The battle scene, drawn by a master, is among the liveliest and most skilful in ancient art; afterwards, prisoners are displayed bleeding on the temple steps, along with a musical parade and scenes of royal women presenting the kingdom with an heir. It is all so *nouveau riche*. And so brief. The paintings were never finished; the scribes never wrote the glorious story; the caption blocks stayed unfilled, a silence more truthful than anything they might have told.

In the year 810 Tikal recorded its final dates.[57] One by one the cities fell still, inscribing no more monuments, until on January 18, 909 (10.4.0.0.0 to the Maya), the last date was carved (at Toniná) and the great machinery of the Long Count calendar ceased to revolve.[58]

What went wrong? As in Rome, all the usual suspects — war, drought, disease, soil exhaustion, invasion, trade disruption, peasant revolt — have been questioned. Some of these are too sudden to account for a collapse that took more than a century. But many of these things would flow from ecological malaise. Again, sediment studies show widespread erosion. There are no goats to blame in this case, but small losses each year still added up to bankruptcy. Stone axes are slower than steel, and hoes gentler than ploughs, but enough of them will do the same job in the end.

The fertility of a rainforest is mainly in the trees. Modern clearing in Amazonia shows that tropical loam can be destroyed in a few years. The Maya understood their soils and conserved them better than today's chainsaw settlers do, but eventually demand overtook supply. David Webster, who has excavated at several major sites and written a recent book on the Maya fall, says this about the greatest of the city-states: "The most convincing collapse explanation we have for the Tikal kingdom is overpopulation and agrarian failure, with all of their attendant political consequences."[59]

His conclusion holds for most of the central lowlands. The ornate Maya city of Copan, which stands in a Honduran valley surrounded by steep hills, fell into a common trap — one that is costing millions of acres around the world today. The city began as a small village on good bottom land beside a river, a rational and harmless settlement pattern at first. But as it grew, it paved over more and more of its best land. Farmers were driven up onto fragile hillside soils whose anchoring timber had been cleared. As the city died, so much silt washed down that whole houses and streets were buried.[60]

Human bones from Classic sites show a growing divide between rich and poor — the wealthy getting taller and heavier while the peasants become stunted. Towards the end, all classes seem to have suffered a general decline in health and life expectancy. If we had Maya mummies to examine, we would probably find them riddled with parasites and the ills of malnutrition, like ancient Egyptians. Webster believes that at the height of Copan's magnificence, during the long reign of King Yax Pasaj, "life expectancy was short, mortality was high, people were often sick, malnourished, and decrepit-looking."[61]

House remains show that in a century and a half, Copan's population had shot up from about 5,000 to 28,000, peaking in A.D. 800; it stayed high for one century, then fell by half in fifty years, then dropped to nearly nothing by A.D. 1200. We can't attribute these figures to mass migration in or out, for much the same pattern occurs throughout the Maya area. The graph, Webster observes, "closely resembles the kind of 'boom and bust' cycle associated with . . . wild animal populations."[62] He might have compared it to something more immediate: Copan's fivefold surge in just a century and a half is exactly the same rate of increase as the modern world's leap from about 1.2 billion in 1850 to 6 billion in 2000.

Some scholars attribute the fall to a severe drought early in the ninth century, a Maya dust bowl. Yet collapse in several areas had already begun by then.[63] During their peak in the eighth century, the great cities of the Maya heartland were running at the limit. They had cashed in all their natural capital. The forest was cut, the fields worn out, the population too high. And the building boom made matters worse, taking more land and timber. Their situation was unstable, vulnerable to any downturn in natural systems. A drought — even if it was no worse than others the Maya had weathered before — would have been more of a finishing blow than a cause.[64]

As the crisis gathered, the response of the rulers was not to seek a new course, to cut back on royal and military expenditures, to put effort into land reclamation through terracing, or to encourage birth control (means of which the Maya may have known). No, they dug in their heels and carried on doing what they had always done, only more so. Their solution was higher pyramids, more power to the kings, harder work for the masses, more foreign wars. In modern terms, the Maya elite became extremists, or ultra-conservatives, squeezing the last drops of profit from nature and humanity.

Of the four cases we've looked at so far, two — Easter Island and Sumer — failed to recover because their ecologies were unable to regenerate. The other two, Rome and the Maya, collapsed heavily in their heartlands, where ecological demand had been highest, but left remnant societies whose descendants have come down to modern times. During a thousand years of low population, the land in both countries managed to recover — helped by volcanic ashfalls and pandemics.[65] Italy is no Easter Island, and Guatemala is no Sumer.[66]

There's a riddle here: Why, if civilizations so often destroy themselves, has the overall experiment of civilization done so well? If Rome couldn't feed itself in the long run, how is it possible that for every person on earth in Roman times, there are thirty here today?

Natural regeneration and human migration are part of the answer. Ancient civilizations were local, feeding on particular ecologies. As one fell, another would be rising elsewhere. Large tracts of the planet were still very lightly settled. A fast film of the earth from space would show civilizations breaking out like forest fires in one region after another. Some were isolated and spontaneous; others were carried from place to place across the centuries, sparks on the cultural wind. A few flared a second time in a good place after a long fallow, rekindling from old coals.

A second answer is that while most civilizations have outrun natural limits and collapsed within a thousand years or so, not *all* have. Egypt and China were able to keep burning, without using up their natural fuel, for more than 3,000 years. What made them different?

Egypt, as Herodotus wrote, was "the gift of the Nile," her fields watered and her soils refreshed each year by a layer of flood-borne silt. Desert hills hemming the river on both sides showed from the start what the limits of tillage would be; there were no wooded slopes or jungles to tempt a population boom on fleeting soils.[67] The Nile and its delta offered only 15,000 square miles[68] of cropland, an area the size of Holland drawn out in the shape of a lotus with its head touching the sea. Egypt's farming methods were simple — as conservative as the culture itself —and worked with, rather than against, the natural water cycle.[69] The Nile valley's narrowness and drainage slowed the salt build-up that poisoned Sumer; and unlike the Maya and ourselves, ancient Egyptians generally knew better than to build on farmland.[70]

Egypt's population growth was unusually slow. Throughout the Pharaonic, Roman, and Arabic periods, it stayed well below world average — taking 3,000 years, from the Old Kingdom to Cleopatra's time, to rise from under 2 million to 6 million, and rising no further until the nineteenth century, when modern irrigation began.[71] This tells us that 6 million people, or 400 per square mile,[72] was the carrying capacity of the Nile farmland, a limit grimly enforced by famine when the river faltered and by high levels of waterborne disease.[73] Nature made Egypt live within its means. But Egypt's means were those of a remittance man — topped up each year by the Nile at the expense of other farming peoples upstream in the Ethiopian highlands.

China also received more than her fair share of topsoil, though it had come as a lump-sum deposit rather than a yearly allowance. Long before farming began, dry winds blowing across the Eurasian landmass had picked up topsoil exposed by retreating glaciers and dropped it on China in the form of loess, a lion-coloured earth that gives the Yellow River its name. The deposits lie hundreds of feet thick in fertile plateaux carved here and there into precipitous ravines or spread out in alluvial plains below. This land was almost endlessly forgiving, with erosion merely exposing new layers of good earth.[74] Civilization in China began more than a thousand years after Egypt, but soon overtook it in scale and spread into other climatic zones. At the height of the Han Empire, China ruled 50 million people from Mongolia to Vietnam — the same number as its contemporary and distant trading partner, Rome.[75]

The Han Dynasty's fall in the third century A.D. was more political than ecological in cause. China was soon revitalized with new ideas from India and the spread in the south of rice-paddy farming, one of the most productive agrarian systems ever devised.

Even so, if we were to scrutinize Egypt and China more closely, we would find them less steady than they seem from afar. Around 2000 B.C., for instance, a series of low Nile floods sparked famine and revolts, toppling the Old Kingdom. In China, too, hungry peasants rebelled against oppressive elites. On one occasion fraught with social irony, they dug into an emperor's tomb, stole weapons from the hands of his terracotta army, and used them to overthrow the Ch'in dynasty.

Despite such upsets, and the recurring scythes of famine and disease, the generous ecologies of Egypt and China allowed revival before the culture lost its headway.[76]

"A culture," said W. H. Auden, "is no better than its woods." Civilizations have developed many techniques for making the earth produce more food — some sustainable, others not. The lesson I read in the past is this: that the health of land and water — and of woods, which are the keepers of water — can be the only lasting basis for any civilization's survival and success.

Eventually, from rags of woodland left in buffer zones between the fallen city-states, the Maya jungle grew back. A family squatting in an empty palace at Tikal — as some did in the aftermath — would have seen thorns and saplings reclaiming the old fields, seen the bush edging into the streets, and heard the wary voices of returning wildlife. Reflecting on the slow revival of fertility and its eventual promise, they might have agreed with Kafka: "There is hope; though not for us."

V

THE REBELLION OF THE TOOLS

I HAVE A WEAKNESS for cynical graffiti. One relevant to the hazards of progress is this: "Each time history repeats itself, the price goes up." The collapse of the first civilization on earth, the Sumerian, affected only half a million people. The fall of Rome affected tens of millions. If ours were to fail, it would, of course, bring catastrophe on billions.

So far we've looked at four ancient societies — Sumer, Rome, the Maya, Easter Island — which, in roughly a thousand years each, wore out their welcome from nature and collapsed. I've also mentioned two exceptions, Egypt and China, who achieved a run of 3,000 years or more.

Joseph Tainter, in his book on past collapses, nicknames three kinds of trouble the Runaway Train, the Dinosaur, and the House of Cards. These usually act together.[1] The Sumerians' irrigation was certainly a runaway train, a disastrous course from which they could not deviate; the rulers' failure to tackle the problem qualifies them as dinosaurs, and the civilization's swift and irreparable fall shows it to have been a house of cards.

Much the same can be said of the other failures. We are faced by something deeper than mistakes at any particular time or place. The invention of agriculture is itself a runaway train, leading to vastly expanded populations but seldom solving the food problem because of two inevitable (or nearly inevitable) consequences. The first is biological: the population grows until it hits the bounds of the food supply. The second is social: all civilizations become hierarchical; the upward concentration of wealth ensures that there can never be enough to go around. The economist Thomas Malthus explored the first dilemma, and thinkers from Christ to Marx have touched on the second. As the Chinese saying has it: "A peasant must stand a long time on the hillside with his mouth open before a roast duck flies in."

Civilization is an experiment, a very recent way of life in the human career, and it has a habit of walking into what I am calling progress traps. A small village on good land beside a river is a good idea; but when the village grows into a city and paves over the good land, it becomes a bad idea. While prevention might have been easy, a cure may be impossible: a city isn't easily moved. This human inability to foresee — or to watch out for — long-range consequences may be inherent to our kind, shaped by the millions of years when we lived from hand to mouth by hunting and gathering. It may also be little more than a mix of inertia, greed, and foolishness encouraged by the shape of the social pyramid. The concentration of power at the top of large-scale societies gives the elite a vested interest in the status quo; they continue to prosper in darkening times long after the environment and general populace begin to suffer.

Yet despite the wreckage of past civilizations littering the earth, the overall experiment of civilization has continued to spread and grow. The numbers (insofar as they can be estimated) break down as follows: a world population of about 200 million at Rome's height, in the second century A.D.; about 400 million by 1500, when Europe reached the Americas[2]; one billion people by 1825, at the start of the Coal Age; 2 billion by 1925, when the Oil Age gets under way; and 6 billion by the year 2000. Even more startling than the growth is the acceleration. Adding 200 million after Rome took thirteen centuries; adding the last 200 million took only three years.[3]

We tend to regard our age as exceptional, and in many ways it is. But the parochialism of the present — the way our eyes follow the ball and not the game — is dangerous. Absorbed in the here and now, we lose sight of our course through time, forgetting to ask ourselves Paul Gauguin's final question: *Where are we going?* If so many previous ages ran into natural limits and crashed, how has our runaway train (if that's what it is) been able to keep on gathering speed?

I suggested earlier that the Chinese and Egyptian civilizations were exceptionally long-lived because nature gave them lavish subsidies of extra topsoil, brought in by wind and water from elsewhere. But some credit must go to human ingenuity. The number of mouths an acre of land can support, and the length of time it can go on supporting them, does not depend only on natural fertility. Civilization did get better at farming as it went along. The mixed farm, with the use of animal and human dung on ploughed land, proved endlessly sustainable on the heavy loams of northern Europe. Crop rotation and use of "green manure" (the ploughing under of nitrogen-fixing plants) raised yields considerably in early modern times. The Asian development of wet rice cultivation was highly productive, and its precisely levelled paddy fields encouraged sustainable tillage of hillsides. The Islamic civilization of Spain not only handed down Classical learning to late-mediaeval Europe, it also repaired the eroded landscape Rome had left by building olive terraces and advanced irrigation schemes. In the Andes, the Incas and pre-Incas built an efficient mountain agriculture on flights of stone terraces watered by glacial streams and fertilized with guano, which they mined from ancient seabird rookeries on arid coastal islands. Studies of Andean terracing in use for the past 1,500 years show no loss of fertility.[4]

Such steady improvements in farming methods can explain a steady rise in population, but not the great boom of the past few centuries. Mechanization and sanitation may account for later stages of the boom, but not its beginnings, which pre-date farm machinery and public health. The take-off point was about a century after Columbus. This was when the strange fruits of the

Spanish conquest began to be digested. Europe received the greatest subsidy of all when half a planet, fully developed but almost unprotected, fell suddenly into its hands.

If America had been a wilderness, the invaders wouldn't have got much out of it for a long time. Every field would have had to be won from the forest, every crop imported and adapted, every mine discovered, every road cut across trackless desert and ranges. But this unknown world had had its own Neolithic Revolutions, and had built a series of civilizations on a rich agrarian base.

The three Americas formed a complex world much like Asia, teeming with 80 to 100 million people — between a fifth and a fourth of the human race. The most powerful polities in 1500 were the Aztec Empire, a city-state system dominated by the conurbation known as Mexico, and the Inca Empire, or Tawantinsuyu,[5] stretching three thousand miles[6] down the spine of the Andes and Pacific coast. Each of these had roughly 20 million people — midway in scale between ancient Egypt and Rome.[7] With a quarter-million citizens, the Aztec capital was then the biggest city in the Americas and one of the half dozen biggest in the world. The Inca Empire was less urban but tightly organized, with 14,000 miles[8] of paved roads, a command economy, and vast terracing and irrigation projects built by a labour-tax system, rather than slavery. Though hardly a workers' paradise, it soon began to look like one to survivors under Spanish rule.[9] Both these empires were young, the heirs of others, and might have had centuries ahead of them if no outsiders had arrived.[10] But they awaited intruders like orchards of ripe fruit.

The environmental historians Alfred Crosby and William McNeill showed in the 1970s that the New World's true conquerors were germs: mass killers such as smallpox, bubonic plague, influenza, and measles. These arrived for the first time with the Europeans (who had resistance to them) and acted like biological weapons, killing the rulers and at least half the populations of Mexico and Peru in the first wave.[11] "The miraculous triumphs" of the conquistadors, Crosby wrote, "are in large part the triumphs of the [smallpox] virus."[12] Despite their guns and horses, the Spaniards did not achieve any major conquests on the mainland until *after* a smallpox pandemic had swept through. Before that, the Maya, Aztecs, Incas, and Floridians all repelled the first efforts to invade them.[13]

Some years ago, the Pentagon came up with plans for a Strangelovian weapon called the neutron bomb, to be let off high over Russian cities so that a searing blast of radiation would kill all the people but leave the property unharmed.[14] The European invaders of America had a weapon of exactly this effect in disease. Let nobody say the New World went down without a fight: the battles for Mexico and Cusco were among the hardest fought in history.[15] But once the epidemiological veil was torn, the people became too few to defend what their ancestors had built up for 10,000 years. "They died in heaps like bedbugs," wrote a Spanish friar in Mexico.[16]

Except for the Great Plains and its cold regions, even North America was not wild in 1500. Hollywood may have persuaded us that the "typical" Indian was a buffalo hunter. But all temperate zones of the United States, from the Southwest to the Southeast and north to Missouri, Ohio, and the Great Lakes, were thickly settled by farming peoples. When the Pilgrims arrived in Massachusetts, the Indians had died out so recently that the whites found empty cabins, winter corn, and cleared fields waiting for their use: a foretoken of the settlers' parasitic advance across the continent. "Europeans did not find a wilderness here," the American historian Francis Jennings has written, "they made one."[17]

For the Spanish, disease was a better weapon than a neutron bomb because just enough Amerindians survived to work the mines.[18] The Aztec and Inca treasures were only a down payment on all the gold and silver that would flow across the Atlantic for centuries.[19] Karl Marx was among the first economists to see that, financially, the Industrial Revolution begins with Atahuallpa's gold. "An indispensable condition for the establishment of manufacturing industry," he said in 1847, "was the accumulation of capital facilitated by the discovery of America and the importation of its precious metals."[20] The Genoese and German bankers who underwrote Spain's empire were awash in bullion looking for something to do. Much found its way to northern Europe, financing shipbuilding, gun foundries, and other imperial ventures. Much also went on European wars — and wars between peers are mothers of invention. In a way Mao Zedong didn't intend, power would indeed grow from the barrel of a gun: from the cannon's "reeking tube" descends the cylinder of the steam and petrol engines.

Gold and silver formed just one side of a transatlantic triangle of loot, land, and labour. The New World's widowed acres — and above all its crops — would prove far more valuable than its metal in the long run. At their Thanksgiving dinners, devout Americans thank their God for feeding them in a "wilderness." They then devour a huge meal of turkey, maize, beans, squash, pumpkin, and potatoes. All these foods had been developed over thousands of years by New World civilizations. It is also hard to imagine curry without chiles, Italian food without tomatoes, the Swiss and Belgians with no chocolate, Hawaiians without pineapples, Africans without cassava, and the British with fish but no chips.

Besides their effect on diet, the new crops brought a dramatic rise in output — in Africa and Asia, as well as in Europe. Maize and potatoes are about twice as productive as wheat and barley, needing only half the land and workforce to yield the same amount of food.[21] Populations rose and large numbers of people left the farm, generating labour surpluses from Britain to the Gold Coast.[22] In the north these people ended up in mills and factories, while in Africa they became foreign exchange for manufactured goods, especially guns.[23]

Europeans shipped Africans across the Atlantic to replace indigenous Americans, and made them grow sugar, cotton, and coffee for European cities.[24] Later, Europe also began exporting surplus people — to fill the prairies and pampas, which proved ideal for growing wheat and barley. With the invention of farm machinery, the Old World grains became less labour-intensive. And with the rediscovery and worldwide use of guano — another gift of Inca agriculture — crop yields soared.[25] When the guano deposits and other natural fertilizers were exhausted, commercial farming became almost entirely dependent on chemical fertilizers made from oil and gas. Fossil energy not only powers but feeds the modern world. We are literally eating oil.[26]

In 1991 William McNeill concluded: "The modern surge of population, sustained in large part by the new crops, is still going on, with drastic but unforeseeable ecological results."[27] In the thirteen years since he wrote that, a billion more people have appeared on earth — the same as the whole population at the beginning of mechanization in 1825. One billion may be close to the number who could feed themselves indefinitely by muscle power if industrial civilization were to fail.

We will never know when, where, or even whether the Industrial Revolution would have happened had America not existed. My guess is that it would — but later, more gradually, and in a different way. It might have begun in China rather than in Europe, or in both.[28] But that is for the "what if" school of history. All we can say is that things would have moved more slowly and been very different. The world we have today is the gift of the New World.

The New World, then, really was Eldorado. It was also Utopia. Early reports of Amazonian societies had influenced Sir Thomas More's book of that name, published in 1516. A century later, the bestselling writer Garcilaso de la Vega, who was half Inca, promoted his mother's fallen empire as the ideal state.[29] In North America, the influence was more direct, a matter of daily example. The early frontier culture was a hybrid, a place where Indians grew orchards and whites took up scalping. Settlers fought, traded, and intermarried with self-governing native peoples who practised social equality, free debate in council, and the rule of consensus. "Their whole constitution breathes nothing but liberty!" wrote James Adair, of the Cherokees, in 1775. Benjamin Franklin had made similar observations about the Iroquois Confederacy, which he urged the Thirteen Colonies to emulate.[30] The whites were particularly impressed by the way dissenters would simply leave the rest of their nation and form an independent group. Here — spread before the eyes of colonists resentful of a distant crown — were freedom, democracy, and the right of secession.

It was, and still is, not well known that these native democracies were largely a post-Columbian development, blooming in the open spaces left by the great dying of the 1500s. Most of the eastern farming "tribes" were remnants of once-powerful chiefdoms. Had the English come to America before the demographic collapse, they would have found a more familiar social structure: lords who lived in great houses atop hundred-foot[31] earthen pyramids, were carried about on litters, and were buried with slaves and concubines.[32] The smallpox virus, having overthrown such societies along with the Aztec and Inca empires, therefore played a precursory role in the

American Revolution. Most uprisings are sparked by want; the American rebels were inspired by plenty — by Indian land and Indian ideals. In more than one way, Franklin's countrymen became, as he called them, "white savages."

The American Revolution in turn influenced the French Revolution, which had its own white savagery known as the Terror. Governments keen to avoid more of the same began broadening the franchise throughout the following century. A measure of participation filtered grudgingly down the social pyramid, while the new industrial economy nourished a growing middle class.[33]

We in the lucky countries of the West now regard our two-century bubble of freedom and affluence as normal and inevitable; it has even been called the "end" of history, in both a temporal and teleological sense.[34] Yet this new order is an anomaly: the opposite of what usually happens as civilizations grow. Our age was bankrolled by the seizing of half a planet, extended by taking over most of the remaining half, and has been sustained by spending down new forms of natural capital, especially fossil fuels. In the New World, the West hit the biggest bonanza of all time. And there won't be another like it — not unless we find the civilized Martians of H. G. Wells, complete with the vulnerability to our germs that undid them in his *War of the Worlds*.[35]

The experiment of civilization has long had its doubters, even in times when change moved too slowly for most people to remark. The tales of Icarus, Prometheus, and Pandora illustrate the risks of being too clever by half, a theme also known to Genesis.[36] Perhaps the most insightful ancient story of this kind — particularly as it comes from a civilization that had suffered collapse — is the "Rebellion of the Tools" in the Maya creation epic, the *Popol Vuh*,[37] where human beings are overthrown by their farm and household implements:

> And all [those things] began to speak. . . . "You . . . shall feel our strength. We shall grind and tear your flesh to pieces," said their grinding stones. . . . At the same time, their griddles and pots spoke: "Pain and suffering you have caused us. . . . You burned us as if we felt no pain. Now you shall feel it, we shall burn you."[38]

As the Cuban writer Alejo Carpentier pointed out, this is our first explicit warning of the threat in the machine.

Such warnings became common in the nineteenth century, when, for the first time ever, wrenching technical and social change was felt within a single lifetime. In 1800, the cities had been small, the air and water relatively clean — which is to say that it would give you cholera, not cancer. Nothing moved faster than by wind or limb. The sound of machinery was almost unknown. A person from 1600 transported to 1800 could have made his way around quite easily. But by 1900, there were motor cars on the streets and electric trains beneath them; movies were flickering on screens; earth's age was reckoned in millions of years, and Albert Einstein was writing his Special Theory of Relativity.

Early in the century, Mary Shelley pondered the new science with her *Frankenstein*. And Charles Dickens gave the social costs of industry a scalding and prescient critique in *Hard Times*, asking whether "the Good Samaritan was a Bad Economist," and foreseeing the new religion of the bottom line: "Every inch of the existence of mankind, from birth to death," he wrote in 1854, "was to be a bargain across a counter."[39]

In his 1872 novel, *Erewhon* (an anagram of "nowhere"), Samuel Butler created a remote civilization that had industrialized long before Europe, but where the effects of progress had sparked a Luddite revolution. The great danger, wrote an Erewhon radical, was not so much the existing machines as the speed at which they were evolving: if not stopped in time, they might develop language, reproduce themselves, and subjugate mankind. Butler was sending up Darwinism here, but the anxieties stirred by the panting monsters of the Steam Age were real enough. Years before he became prime minister, the young Benjamin Disraeli had anticipated *Erewhon*'s fears in his novel *Coningsby*: "The mystery of mysteries," he wrote, "is to view machines making machines, a spectacle that fills the mind with curious and even awful speculation."[40]

As the Victorian age rushed on, many writers began to ask, "Where are we going?" If so much was happening so quickly in *their* century, what might happen in the next? Butler, Wells, William Morris, Richard Jefferies, and many others mixed fantasy, satire, and allegory, creating a genre known as the scientific romance.

In *The Time Machine* of 1895, Wells sent a traveller to a distant future where the human race has split into two species, the Eloi and the Morlocks. The Eloi are a sybaritic upper class living brainlessly on the industrial toil of the Morlocks, never guessing that these underground sub-humans — seemingly their slaves — are in fact raising them for meat.

In his *News from Nowhere*, William Morris dreamt up a *post*-industrial New Age — a pre-Raphaelite Utopia of honest workmanship, good design, and free love — from which he attacked the first great wave of globalization, the world market ruled by the steamship, the telegraph, and the British Empire:

> The happiness of the workman at his work, his most elementary comfort and bare health. . . . did not weigh a grain of sand in the balance against this dire necessity of "cheap production" of things, a great part of which were not worth producing at all. . . . The whole community was cast into the jaws of this ravening monster, the World-Market.

While we may learn from the past, we don't seem to learn much. That last generation before the First World War — the time of the young Einstein, Oscar Wilde, and Joseph Conrad's novel of terrorism, *The Secret Agent* — was in many ways a time like ours: an old century grown tired; a new century in which moralities and certainties were withering, bombers were lurking in the shadows, and industrialists declaiming from their mansions that unfettered free enterprise would bring a New Jerusalem to all.

More thoughtful observers sensed that change was running out of control, and began to fear that with the powers of industry, mankind had found the means to suicide. They saw jingoistic nation-states engaged in an arms race. They saw social exploitation and vast urban slums, contaminated air and water, and "civilization" being conferred on "savages" through the barrels of machine guns.[41]

What if those guns were turned not on Zulus or Sioux but on other Europeans? What if the degradation of the slums caused degeneration of the human race? What, exactly, was the *point* of all this economic output if, for so many people, it meant deracination, misery, and filth? By the end of his voyage, Wells's Time Traveller regards civilization as "only a foolish heaping that must inevitably . . . destroy its makers in the end."

No doubt many will say that we stand here to prove those gloomy Victorians wrong. But do we? They may have been wrong on the details they imagined for our times, but they were right to foresee trouble. Just ahead lay the Great War and 12 million dead,[42] the Russian Revolution, the Great Slump — leading to Hitler, the death camps, the Second World War (with 50 million dead), the atom bomb. And these in turn to the Korean War, the Cold War, the near-fatal Cuban Missile Crisis, Vietnam, Cambodia, Rwanda. Even the most pessimistic Victorian might have been surprised to learn that the twentieth century would slaughter more than 100 million in its wars — twice the entire population of the Roman Empire.[43] The price of history does indeed go up.

The Victorian scientific romances had two modern descendants: mainstream science fiction, and profound social satire set in nightmare futures. The latter includes several of the last century's most important books: Aldous Huxley's *Brave New World*, George Orwell's *Nineteen Eighty-four*, J. M. Coetzee's *Waiting for the Barbarians*, and a number of post-nuclear wastelands, of which Russell Hoban's *Riddley Walker* has to be the masterpiece.

With the nuclear threat fading (maybe), modern apocalyptic novels have revisited concerns first raised before Hiroshima — especially the risks of new technology, and how our species might survive without abandoning its humanity for antlike order. (Perhaps the most disturbing aspect of *Brave New World* was the strong case Huxley made for the devil of order, a case harder to answer now than in 1932.) The clanking monsters of Erewhon have taken subtler forms that threaten the whole biosphere: climate disruption, toxic waste, new pathogens, nano-technology, cybernetics, genetic engineering.

One of the dangers of writing a dystopian satire is how depressing it is when you get things right. Ten years ago I began work on my novel *A Scientific Romance*, a title I chose because I wanted to acknowledge the Victorians, and because my theme was our *amour fou* with science. For satirical purposes, I made what I thought were wild extrapolations from things in the news. I had a character die of mad cow disease, thinking that in the final draft I would probably have to kill her off with something less far-fetched. By the time the book was published in 1997, dozens of people really had died of mad cow.[44] Other elements of the satire — climate change that turns wintry London into a tropical swamp, a race of genetically modified survivors, and a GM grass that doesn't need mowing because it has the self-limiting properties of pubic hair — no longer seem quite the funhouse mirrors they were when I began. Just a few months ago, something more specific came to haunt me. In the jungly ruins of London, my protagonist finds a street blocked off and buildings fortified with concrete slabs. Here, he deduces, an embattled British government must have spent its final days in the 2030s.[45] Earlier this year, I read in the paper that Tony Blair's government is planning to surround the Houses of Parliament with a fifteen foot[46] concrete wall and razor wire.[47]

I don't want to be a prophet, and I certainly don't claim to be. It doesn't take Nostradamus to foresee that walls will go up in times of crisis — though the thickest walls are in the mind. A telling feature of the real mad cow disaster was how long the British government did nothing except hope for the best. In her recent dystopia, *Oryx and Crake*, which concentrates on biotechnology, Margaret Atwood also portrays the collapse of civilization in the near future. One of her characters asks, "As a species we're doomed by hope, then?"[48] By *hope*? Well, yes. Hope drives us to invent new fixes for old messes, which in turn create ever more dangerous messes. Hope elects the politician with the biggest empty promise; and as any stockbroker or lottery seller knows, most of us will take a slim hope over prudent and predictable frugality. Hope, like greed, fuels the engine of capitalism.

John Steinbeck once said that socialism never took root in America because the poor see themselves not as an exploited proletariat but as temporarily embarrassed millionaires. This helps explain why American culture is so hostile to the idea of limits, why voters during the last energy shortage rejected the sweater-wearing Jimmy Carter and elected Ronald Reagan, who scoffed at conservation and told them it was "still morning in America."[49] Nowhere does the myth of progress have more fervent believers.

Marx was surely right when he called capitalism, almost admiringly, "a machine for demolishing limits." Both communism and capitalism are materialist Utopias offering rival versions of an earthly paradise. In practice, communism was no easier on the natural environment. But at least it proposed a sharing of the goods. Capitalism lures us onward like the mechanical hare before the greyhounds, insisting that the economy is infinite and sharing therefore irrelevant. Just enough greyhounds catch a real hare now and then to keep the others running till they drop. In the past it was only the poor who lost this game; now it is the planet.[50]

Those who travelled in their youth, and have gone back to old haunts after twenty or thirty years, can't fail to observe the massive onslaught of progress, whether it be the loss of farms to suburbs, jungles to cattle ranches, rivers to dams, mangroves to shrimp farms, mountains to cement quarries, or coral reefs to condominiums.

We still have differing cultures and political systems,

but at the economic level there is now only one big civilization, feeding on the whole planet's natural capital. We're logging everywhere, fishing everywhere, irrigating everywhere, building everywhere, and no corner of the biosphere escapes our haemorrhage of waste.[51] The twentyfold growth in world trade since the 1970s has meant that hardly anywhere is self-sufficient. Every Eldorado has been looted, every Shangri-La equipped with a Holiday Inn. Joseph Tainter notes this interdependence, warning that "collapse, if and when it comes again, will this time be global. . . . World civilization will disintegrate as a whole."[52]

Experts in a range of fields have begun to see the same closing door of opportunity, begun to warn that these years may be the last when civilization still has the wealth and political cohesion to steer itself towards caution, conservation, and social justice. Twelve years ago, just before the Rio environmental summit that led to the Kyoto Accord on climate change, more than half the world's Nobel laureates warned that we might have only a decade or so left to make our system sustainable. Now, in a report unsuccessfully hushed up by the Bush administration, the Pentagon predicts worldwide famine, anarchy, and warfare "within a generation" should climate change fulfill the more severe projections.[53] And in his 2003 book, *Our Final Century*, Martin Rees of Cambridge University, Astronomer Royal and former president of the British Association for the Advancement of Science, concludes: "The odds are no better than fifty-fifty that our present civilisation . . . will survive to the end of the present century . . . unless all nations adopt low-risk and sustainable policies based on present technology."[54]

Sceptics point to earlier predictions of disaster that weren't borne out. But that is a fool's paradise. Some of our escapes — from nuclear war, for one — have been more by luck than judgment, and are not final.[55] Other problems have been side-stepped but not solved. The food crisis, for example, has merely been postponed by switching to hybrid seed and chemical farming, at great cost to soil health and plant diversity.[56]

Following the attacks of September 11th, 2001, the world's media and politicians focused understandably on terrorism. Two things need to be said here.

First, terrorism is a small threat compared with hunger, disease, or climate change.[57] Three thousand died in the United States that day; 25,000 die *every* day in the world from contaminated water alone. Each year, 20 million children are mentally impaired by malnourishment.[58] Each year, an area of farmland greater than Scotland is lost to erosion and urban sprawl, much of it in Asia.

Second, terrorism cannot be stopped by addressing symptoms and not the cause. Violence is bred by injustice, poverty, inequality, and other violence. This lesson was learnt very painfully in the first half of the twentieth century, at a cost of some 80 million lives.[59] Of course, a full belly and a fair hearing won't stop a fanatic; but they can greatly reduce the number who *become* fanatics.

After the Second World War, a consensus emerged to deal with the roots of violence by creating international institutions and democratically managed forms of capitalism based on Keynesian economics and America's New Deal. This policy, though far from perfect, succeeded in Europe, Japan, and some parts of the Third World.[60] (Remember when we spoke not of a "war on terror" but of a "war on want"?)

To undermine that post-war consensus and return to archaic political patterns is to walk back into the bloody past. Yet that is what the New Right has achieved since the late 1970s, rewrapping old ideas as new and using them to transfer the levers of power from elected governments to unelected corporations — a project sold as "tax-cutting" and "deregulation" by the right's courtiers in the media, of which Canada certainly has its share. The conceit of laissez-faire economics — that if you let the horses guzzle enough oats, something will go through for the sparrows[61] — has been tried many times and has failed many times, leaving ruin and social wreckage.[62]

The revolt against redistribution is killing civilization from ghetto to rainforest.[63] Taxes in most countries have not, in fact, been lowered; they were merely shifted down the income pyramid, and diverted from aid and social programs towards military and corporate ones. The great American judge Oliver Wendell Holmes once said, "I don't mind paying taxes; they buy me civilization." Public confidence in a basic social safety net is essential for lowering birth rates in poor nations, and for a decent society in all nations. The removal of that confidence has set off a free-for-all that is stripping the earth.

During the twentieth century, as I noted earlier in this book, the world's population multiplied by four and the economy by more than forty. If the promise of modernity was even treading water — in other words, if the gap between rich and poor had stayed proportionally the same as it was when Queen Victoria died — all human beings would be ten times better off. Yet the number in abject poverty today is as great as all mankind in 1901.[64]

By the end of the twentieth century, the world's three richest individuals (all of whom were Americans) had a combined wealth greater than that of the poorest forty-eight countries.[65] In 1998, the United Nations calculated that US$40 billion, spent carefully, could provide clean water, sanitation, and other basic needs for the poorest on earth.[66] The figure may be optimistic, and it may have grown in the past six years. But it's still considerably less than the funds already set aside for the obscenely wasteful fantasy of a missile shield that won't work, isn't needed, yet could provoke a new arms race and the militarization of space.

Consider Tainter's three aspects of collapse: the Runaway Train, the Dinosaur, the House of Cards. The rise in population and pollution, the acceleration of technology, the concentration of wealth and power — all are runaway trains, and most are linked together. Population growth is slowing, but by 2050 there will still be 3 billion more on earth. We may be able to feed that many in the short run, but we'll have to raise less meat (which takes ten pounds of food to make one pound of food), and we'll have to spread that food around. What we can't do is keep consuming as we are. Or polluting as we are. We could help countries such as India and China industrialize without repeating our mistakes. But instead we have excluded environmental standards from trade agreements. Like sex tourists with unlawful lusts, we do our dirtiest work among the poor.

If civilization is to survive, it must live on the interest, not the capital, of nature. Ecological markers suggest that in the early 1960s, humans were using about 70 per cent of nature's yearly output; by the early 1980s, we'd reached 100 per cent; and in 1999, we were at 125 per cent.[67] Such numbers may be imprecise, but their trend is clear — they mark the road to bankruptcy.

None of this should surprise us after reading the flight recorders in the wreckage of crashed civilizations; our present behaviour is typical of failed societies at the zenith of their greed and arrogance. This is the dinosaur factor: hostility to change from vested interests, and inertia at all social levels.[68] George Soros, the reformed currency speculator, calls the economic dinosaurs "market fundamentalists." I'm uneasy with this term because so few of them *are* true believers in free markets — preferring monopolies, cartels, and government contracts.[69] But his point is well taken. The idea that the world must be run by the stock market is as mad as any other fundamentalist delusion, Islamic, Christian, or Marxist.

In the case of Easter Island, the statue cult became a self-destructive mania, an ideological pathology. In the United States, market extremism (which one might expect to be purely materialist, and therefore open to rational self-interest) has cross-bred with evangelical messianism to fight intelligent policy on metaphysical grounds. Mainstream Christianity is an altruistic faith, yet this offshoot is actively hostile to the public good: a kind of social Darwinism by people who hate Darwin. President Reagan's secretary of the interior told Congress not to bother with the environment because, in his words, "I don't know how many future generations we can count on until the Lord returns."[70] George W. Bush surrounded himself with similar minds and pulled out of the Kyoto Accord on climate change.[71]

Adolf Hitler once gleefully exclaimed, "What luck for the rulers that the people do not think!" What can we do when the rulers *will* not think?

Civilizations often fall quite suddenly — the House of Cards effect — because as they reach full demand on their ecologies, they become highly vulnerable to natural fluctuations. The most immediate danger posed by climate change is weather instability causing a series of crop failures in the world's breadbaskets. Droughts, floods, fires, and hurricanes are rising in frequency and severity. The pollution surges caused by these — and by wars — add to the gyre of destruction. Medical experts worry that nature may swat us with disease: billions of overcrowded primates, many sick, malnourished, and connected by air travel, are a free lunch waiting for a nimble microbe. "Mother Nature always comes to the rescue of a society stricken with . . . overpopulation," Alfred Crosby sardonically observed, "and her ministrations are never gentle."[72]

The case for reform that I have tried to make is not based on altruism, nor on saving nature for its own sake. I happen to believe that these are moral imperatives, but such arguments cut against the grain of human desire. The most compelling reason for reforming our system is that the system is in no one's interest. It is a suicide machine. All of us have some dinosaur inertia within us, but I honestly don't know what the activist "dinosaurs" — the hard men and women of Big Oil and the far right — think they are doing. They have children and grandchildren who will need safe food and clean air and water, and who may wish to see living oceans and forests. Wealth can buy no refuge from pollution; pesticides sprayed in China condense in Antarctic glaciers and Rocky Mountain tarns. And wealth is no shield from chaos, as the surprise on each haughty face that rolled from the guillotine made clear.

There's a saying in Argentina that each night God cleans up the mess the Argentines make by day. This seems to be what our leaders are counting on. But it won't work. Things are moving so fast that inaction itself is one of the biggest mistakes. The 10,000-year experiment of the settled life will stand or fall by what we do, and don't do, now. The reform that is needed is not anti-capitalist, anti-American, or even deep environmentalist; it is simply the transition from short-term to long-term thinking. From recklessness and excess to moderation and the precautionary principle.

The great advantage we have, our best chance for avoiding the fate of past societies, is that we know about those past societies. We can see how and why they went wrong. *Homo sapiens* has the information to know itself for what it is: an Ice Age hunter only half-evolved towards intelligence; clever but seldom wise.

We are now at the stage when the Easter Islanders could still have halted the senseless cutting and carving, could have gathered the last trees' seeds to plant out of reach of the rats. We have the tools and the means to share resources, clean up pollution, dispense basic health care and birth control, set economic limits in line with natural ones. If we don't do these things now, while we prosper, we will never be able to do them when times get hard. Our fate will twist out of our hands. And this new century will not grow very old before we enter an age of chaos and collapse that will dwarf all the dark ages in our past.

Now is our last chance to get the future right.

NOTES

Introduction to the Anniversary Edition

1. Almost 130 square kilometres.
2. *A Scientific Romance* (Toronto: Knopf Canada, 1997; New York: Picador USA, 1998).
3. At first it was thought *Homo floresiensis* might have lasted until only 12,000 years ago, but current evidence points to their extinction about 50,000 years ago, the time of the great *Homo sapiens sapiens* expansion. In April 2019, news broke that human remains of similar age and size to the Flores folk have been found on Luzon Island in the Philippines.
4. Mathew Warren, "Mum's a Neanderthal, Dad's a Denisovan: First discovery of an ancient human hybrid," *Nature*, August 22, 2018. Of course, the circumstances of her birth are unknown. Was it the result of capture?
5. Readers seeking more on these findings, and on more recent population shifts, will find a thorough (if at times controversial) account in *Who We Are and How We Got*

Here, by David Reich, a leading researcher in the DNA field (New York: Pantheon, 2018).

6. See end of chapter 1.

7. The percentage of Neanderthal ancestry ranges between 1 per cent and 4 per cent nowadays, and is thought to have been higher in the past. Interbreeding seems to have happened at several times and places between 70,000 and 40,000 years ago. Lack of Neanderthal ancestry in most modern Africans suggests that Neanderthals evolved in Eurasia (likely Europe) and never made their way below the Sahara, though they were at times dominant in the Middle East.

8. Percentages of Denisovan ancestry range between 3 per cent and 6 per cent.

9. No *Homo floresiensis* DNA has yet been found; if this changes, their origins and fate will become clearer.

10. The reign of Neanderthals in Europe is now thought to have ended about 39,000 years ago, some 10,000 years earlier than was estimated in 2004. Data for Denisovans are much scarcer. See Reich, *Who We Are*, pp. 24–74.

11. Nine hectares.

12. The Natufians, who occupied the Middle East about 2,000 years earlier, *did* build permanent villages despite being hunter-gatherers. They produced fine stone artefacts such as tools, mortars, and figurines but nothing on a monumental scale.

13. There was no connection; their cultures and crops were wholly different. But each set the foundations for what came later in each region. The new dates underline the independent yet parallel evolution of human society in the Old World and the New.

14. Over 2,000 square kilometres.

15. "Exclusive: Laser Scans Reveal Maya 'Megalopolis' Below Guatemalan Jungle," Tom Clynes, *National Geographic*, February 1, 2018. For comparison, the land inhabited by the ancient (and modern) Maya is smaller than the British Isles, which had about 5 million people in Shakespeare's day.

16. The consumption estimate is deduced from indicators such as world GDP and energy use. Simply put, ecological demand is population times average per capita consumption. The concept of "ecological footprint," expressed as the land area needed to support demand, was first developed by William Rees. William E. Rees, "Ecological footprints and appropriated carrying capacity: what urban economics leaves out," *Environment and Urbanisation* 4, no. 2 (October 1992): 121–30. Since 2004, the rate of population growth has fallen from 1.25 per cent to below 1.1 per cent per year. Growth at 1 per cent is enough to double every 70 years.

17. The World Bank estimated 736 million in extreme poverty in 2018, defined as those below $1.90 a day (in 2011 U.S. dollars). This monetary threshold (about $700 a year) is set very low and likely underestimates the true number of those lacking enough food, clean water, and other basics. Some experts think the poverty line should be set at $7.40 per day (or higher), which would include many working poor in sweatshops, plantations, etc. About 55 per cent of the world's people currently live below the $7.40 threshold. Poverty reduction is slowing, partly because of high population growth in Nigeria and other parts of Africa. See "Decline of Global Extreme Poverty Continues but has Slowed," World Bank press release, September 19, 2018. Also "Bill Gates Says Poverty is Decreasing,"

Guardian, January 29, 2019, by Jason Hickel, author of *The Divide: A Brief Guide to Global Inequality and Its Solution* (London: Heinemann, 2017).

18. This figure, about five times Canada's yearly GDP, is *known* wealth, excluding sums hidden in tax havens by billionaires and multimillionaires, estimated by *Forbes* (September 15, 2017) to be at least a tenth of world yearly GDP.

19. From *Collected Writings of John Maynard Keynes,* vol. 4, *A Tract on Monetary Reform* (Cambridge: Cambridge University Press, 1978), 65. See *Keynes,* by Peter Clarke (London: Bloomsbury, 2009).

20. Estimates vary slightly, depending on methods and criteria. This is drawn from "The biomass distribution on Earth," by Yinon M. Bar-On, Rob Phillips, and Ron Milo, in *Proceedings of the National Academy of Sciences* 115, no. 25 (June 19, 2018), pp. 6506–11. There are not enough data to pinpoint when humans and livestock first reached 4 per cent; about 1,000 years ago, give or take several centuries, seems reasonable. However, we can be certain that at the dawn of farming 10,000 years ago, there were only a few million people on Earth and no livestock but dogs. The human proportion would then have been well below 0.1 per cent.

21. For estimates, see the British Institute for Public Policy Research, reported by BBC World News, "Environment in Multiple Crises," February 12, 2019.

22. This slogan is from an activist's placard. School strikes began in Sweden, inspired by sixteen-year-old Greta Thunberg, and have since spread to many European countries and beyond.

23. "Worldwide decline of the entomofauna: A review of its

drivers," by Francisco Sánchez-Bayo and Kris A.G. Wyck-huys, *Biological Conservation* 232 (April 2019).

24. "Summary for Policymakers of IPCC Special report on Global Warming," issued October 8, 2018.

25. For arguments that this momentum is inherent to capital-ism, see Ronald Wright, *What Is America?* (Toronto: Knopf Canada, 2008), and Naomi Klein, *This Changes Everything* (Toronto: Knopf Canada, 2014).

26. The *Economist* of January 2018 noted that life expectancy in the USA had declined two years in a row.

27. "World's 26 richest people own as much as poorest 50%, says Oxfam," article by Larry Elliott (*Guardian*, January 21, 2019) on the Oxfam Davos report.

28. For three decades after the Second World War, tax rates on top earners never fell below 70 per cent in the United States or Britain, and at times surpassed 90 per cent. This was accepted as needful for the common good: not only for rebuilding after the war but for preventing the desper-ation and extremism that had caused that war and might otherwise lead to another. For a recent analysis of income disparity, see *World Inequality Report 2018*, coordinated by Thomas Piketty (author of *Capital in the Twenty-first Cen-tury*) and others.

29. See *Ten Arguments for Deleting Your Social Media Accounts Right Now* (New York: Henry Holt, 2018), by Jaron Lanier, himself a virtual-reality pioneer and resident Silicon Val-ley critic, who writes, "We're all lab animals now."

I: Gauguin's Questions

1. Unable to afford real canvas, Gauguin painted his master-piece on a length of jute sacking.

2. Quoted in Gavan Daws, *A Dream of Islands* (Honolulu: Mutual Publishing, 1980).

3. Sidney Pollard, *The Idea of Progress: History and Society* (London: C. A. Watts, 1968), p. 9ff.

4. Ibid.

5. Not only religious ones. Victorian archaeology defined technical advance in terms of metals, but the Classical world had drawn the opposite conclusion, seeing only a slide into cheapness and corruptibility — from an age of gold to one of bronze and lastly iron.

6. Ronald Wright, *Stolen Continents: Conquest and Resistance In the Americas* (Boston: Houghton Mifflin, 1992), p. 5.

7. American Cold Warriors of the last century used to threaten to "bomb the Soviets back into the Stone Age." Whether the Russians uttered the same threat, I don't know. But it was certainly a credible one. Even if a nuclear "exchange" (as the euphemism went) failed to extinguish all higher forms of life, it would have ended civilization worldwide. No crops worth eating would grow in a nuclear winter.

8. See Francis Fukuyama, *The End of History and the Last Man* (New York: Free Press, 1992).

9. Alexander Pope, *An Essay on Criticism*, 1711; Thomas Henry Huxley, *On Elementary Instruction in Physiology*, 1877.

10. Quoted in Robert J. Wenke, *Patterns in Prehistory* (Oxford: Oxford University Press, 1980), p. 79.

11. William Shakespeare, *Hamlet*, act 2, scene 2.

12. Ibid., *As You Like It*, act 4, scene 1.

13. Quoted in Glyn Daniel, *The Idea of Prehistory* (Harmondsworth, UK: Pelican, 1962), p. 19.

14. Newton, basing his calculations on the speed at which a mass of iron cools down, had already suspected that the earth was at least 50,000 years old, and the eighteenth-

century French thinkers Benoit de Maillet and George-Louis Leclerc de Buffon opted for far greater estimates, but their calculations gained little acceptance. See Martin Gorst, *Measuring Eternity: The Search for the Beginning of Time* (New York: Broadway Books, 2001), pp. 93–121.

15. The physicist Lord Kelvin fought a rearguard action on the grounds that the sun could not be old enough for Darwin's time scale, but this was widely doubted and eventually disproved.

16. His words were not transcribed at the time. Accounts of what was said differ somewhat but agree on the gist.

17. Gorst, *Measuring Eternity*, p. 204.

18. H. G. Wells et al., *The Science of Life*, vol. 2 (New York: Doubleday, 1929), pp. 422–23. His co-author Julian Huxley was a grandson of Darwin's champion, Thomas Huxley.

19. Northrop Frye, "Humanities in a New World" in *Three Lectures* (Toronto: University of Toronto Press, 1958), p. 23. Some experts see speech as quite a recent phenomenon, but I think it much more likely to have had a very long development, gaining complexity in step with the brain. Many of the differences between ape and human brains are in regions that govern aspects of speech. See chapter 2, note 11, below.

20. Rosny was born in Brussels in 1856, worked as journalist in England, and moved in 1886 to Paris, where he became president of the Académie Goncourt.

21. A 400,000-year-old beach hut at Terra Amata, in southern France, seems to have a hearth, while there are "hints of fire use" in Africa from a million years before that. Ian Tattersall, *The Last Neanderthal: The Rise, Success, and Mysterious Extinction of Our Closest Human Relatives* (New York: Westview Press, 1999), p. 72.

22. See, for example, Loren Eiseley's 1954 essay "Man the Firemaker" in *The Star Thrower* (New York: Harcourt Brace Jovanovich, 1978), pp. 45–52.

23. Ibid., p. 49.

24. Genetic data suggest that at one point, "our species became as endangered as the mountain gorilla is today . . . reduced to only about 10,000 adults." Christopher Stringer and Robin McKie, *African Exodus: The Origins of Modern Humanity* (New York: Henry Holt/John Macrae, 1997), p. 11. At the start of the Upper Palaeolithic, about 35,000 years ago, Stringer estimates that *Homo sapiens* had "a breeding population of at least 300,000." Ibid., p. 163.

25. For the Out of Africa hypothesis, see Stringer and McKie, *African Exodus*. For opposing views, see recent works by M. Wolpoff, G. A. Clark, J. Relethford, and F. H. Smith. For a balanced overview, see Richard Leakey and Roger Lewin, *Origins Reconsidered: In Search of What Makes Us Human* (New York: Doubleday, 1992).

26. Animal species as different from one another as horses, zebras, and donkeys can interbreed, as can lions and tigers, even though the crosses are seldom fertile. The evolutionary gap in such cases is almost certainly wider than between many so-called species of early humans.

27. From H. G. Wells, *The Outline of History*, taken by William Golding as the epigraph of *The Inheritors*, 1955.

28. The case made by W. Arens in *The Man-Eating Myth: Anthropology and Anthropophagy* (New York: Oxford University Press, 1979) that there are no well-documented cases of cannibalism (except survival cannibalism) does not stand up. While many accusations of the practice were, as he claims, unfounded propaganda from rival ethnic groups, there is also abundant hard evidence —

butchered bone, special utensils, sound ethnographic and historical data — for both ritual and gourmet cannibalism, especially in the Pacific. There are also numerous documented cases of atrocity cannibalism from European wars in Reformation times and African wars between 1960 and the present.

29. Tattersall, *Last Neanderthal*, p. 77. A useful book, though Tattersall holds the view that Neanderthals were a separate species with no modern descendants.

30. Erik Trinkaus and Pat Shipman, *The Neanderthals: Changing the Image of Mankind* (New York: Knopf, 1993), p. 6. These authors give a good summary of the conflicting evidence. For a more recent discussion of human origins and the Neanderthal problem, see *General Anthropology* 7, no. 2 (Spring 2001), a newsletter published by the American Anthropological Association.

31. Those who take this view use the classification *Homo sapiens neanderthalensis* for Neanderthals and that of *Homo sapiens sapiens* for Cro-Magnons and other modern humans.

32. Ornella Semino and other geneticists conclude that more than 80 per cent of the modern European gene pool has Upper Palaeolithic ancestry, while 20 per cent comes from Neolithic farmers who arrived much later from the Middle East. See *Science*, November 10, 2000.

33. An indicator of this is that early Neanderthal skulls are generally less robust than later ones. Tattersall, *Last Neanderthal*, p. 147.

34. Christopher Stringer, "The Evolution of Modern Humans: Where Are We Now?" *General Anthropology* 7, no. 2 (Spring 2001).

35. This cultural phase, called the Chatelperronian, is fully apparent by 36,000 years ago, at Saint-Césaire in western

France. Tattersall, *Last Neanderthal*, p. 145. See also Francis B. Harold, "The Case Study of the Chatelperronian," *General Anthropology* 7, no. 2 (Spring 2001). From analysing living floors and site structure, Donald Henry and his co-authors conclude that "putative linkages between [Neanderthal] biology and behaviour . . . can be dismissed" (Donald Henry et al., "Human Behavioral Organization in the Middle Paleolithic: Were Neanderthals Different?" *American Anthropologist* 106, no. 1 (March 2004): 29); they find no reason to think that Neanderthal and Cro-Magnon groups differed in cognitive ability.

36. Quoted in Leakey and Lewin, *Origins Reconsidered*, p. 280ff (caption to plate 4).

37. The studies were based on partial sequences from poorly preserved material. See John H. Relethford, "New Views on Neanderthal DNA," *General Anthropology* 7, no. 2 (Spring 2001).

38. The Portuguese site is Lagar Velho and the bones are about 24,000 years old.

39. Trinkaus and Shipman (*Neanderthals*, p. 415) write that in central Europe, "there is abundant evidence of continuous evolution, genetic admixture and interbreeding between resident Neanderthals and the early modern humans who were filtering in slowly from the Levant." See a curiously moving memoir by Loren Eiseley (*Star Thrower*, pp. 139–152) for his eloquent conviction that Neanderthals are still among us. Tattersall, who holds the view that Neanderthals were an entirely separate species, writes that the Neanderthal bun (the occipital torus) and its associated valley (the suprainiac depression) are features "unique to Neanderthals" (Tattersall, *Last Neanderthal*, p. 118). But I have one all the same.

40. In a similar way, many descendants of American Indians, Australian Aboriginals, Africans, and other displaced people are submerged in "white" populations largely unaware of their mixed ancestry.

II: The Great Experiment

1. Evidence is growing that people reached the Americas (the last continent to be settled) earlier than the established estimate of 15,000 years ago. It is likely that watercraft were involved — for island-hopping and moving down coastlines — in addition to the land routes across the Bering causeway during glaciations. Greater Australia (including New Guinea) was an island throughout the Ice Age, yet people got there by island-hopping 40,000 to 60,000 years ago.

2. This event, which happened 65 million years ago, was probably the fifth of its kind. Since complex life appeared, the earth seems to have averaged one cosmic bombshell every hundred million years. Many scientists regard the human impact on the biosphere as the beginning of a "sixth extinction." See, for example, Rees, *Our Final Century*, p. 100ff.

3. The double *sapiens* is used by those who believe that Neanderthals and Cro-Magnons were variants within the same species — see chapter 1. If 30 to 35 billion is the total of humans and hominids who have ever lived, at least 20–25 billion of these lived in civilized societies during the past three millennia. In other words, two-thirds of us (or more) have lived during the last one thousandth of the human career, and about a fifth or sixth of all are living now.

4. A few exceptions to the farming definition can be argued for regions where wild food resources were unusually

plentiful and predictable. The best historic example of a nascent civilization without agriculture is the Northwest coast of North America, but such cases may have been more numerous in the distant past. Scholars used to insist on specific criteria, such as writing, when defining the state of civilization. Modern definitions are more flexible, and look at the overall scale and complexity of a culture. See Bruce Trigger, *Early Civilizations: Ancient Egypt in Context* (Cairo: American University in Cairo Press, 1993), p. 7.

5. George Gilmer, governor of Georgia, said in the 1830s: "Treaties were expedients by which . . . savage people were induced . . . to yield up what civilized people had the right to possess." The "removal," or ethnic cleansing, of the Cherokees at this time included the use of forced marches and concentration camps for civilians, in which thousands died; see Wright, *Stolen Continents*, chap. 14. (The term "concentration camp" was coined by the British during the Boer War.) See Sven Lindqvist, *Exterminate All the Brutes*, trans. Joan Tate (London: Granta Books, 1996), for the case that the Nazi Holocaust and other modern atrocities derive from racist colonial policy, especially in Africa.

6. The Colosseum and other Roman circuses saw bloody sacrifice on a grand scale; during the four-month games of Trajan, 5,000 men and 11,000 animals were slaughtered.

7. Some estimates go much higher, especially if war-induced famine and disease are included.

8. Gandhi was hardly the "naked fakir" of Churchill's insult, having been a law student in London during the 1890s.

9. Henry Thoreau's phrase.

10. On the eve of the Steam Age in 1825, the world's population was about one billion; if industrial civilization were

to collapse, the sustainable population would fall back to a similar level. Put bluntly, billions would die.

11. Erich Harth, quoted in Stringer and McKie, *African Exodus* (p. 243). Alfred Crosby, in *Ecological Imperialism: The Biological Expansion of Europe 900–1900* (Cambridge: Cambridge University Press, 1986), p. 14, writes: "By about 100,000 years ago, the human brain was as large as it is today, which is probably as large as it will ever be."

12. William Golding, *Pincher Martin* (London: Faber and Faber, 1956), p. 190. This novel, published soon after *The Inheritors*, ponders the nature of man in a modern setting: the mind of a seaman torpedoed in the North Atlantic.

13. The bow and arrow may not have appeared until later, but the spearthrower, or launcher (known to archaeologists by its Aztec name, *atlatl*), was almost certainly an Upper Palaeolithic invention. It increases the length and leverage of the human throw, somewhat like a lacrosse stick.

14. The Grotte Chauvet paintings near Avignon, among the oldest yet found in Europe, show sophistication and maturity by 32,000 years ago. Although widely assumed to be the work of early Cro-Magnons, they could also have been done by Neanderthals. However, the dates have been challenged and await further carbon dating (see *Antiquity*, March 2003). The heyday of European cave art came much later — around 17,000 to 15,000 years ago, at Lascaux and Altamira. Probably not seen as "art" by its makers, it was most likely shamanic, intended to worship the powers of nature and increase the game.

15. From here on, I use the shorter version of our name for fluency.

16. A smaller bison survived in North America, of course, as did deer, and the camelids (llama family) in South America.

17. Crosby, in *Ecological Imperialism* (p. 272), writes: "Humans, even if armed only with the torch and with weapons of stone . . . are the most dangerous and unrelenting predators in the world."

18. The mammoths died at Piedmost in the Czech Republic, the horses at Solutré in France, which gives its name to the superb Solutrean point. See William Howells, *Mankind in the Making: The Story of Human Evolution* (London: Secker and Warburg, 1960), p. 206, and Andrew Goudie, *The Human Impact on the Natural Environment* (Oxford: Blackwell, 2000), p. 145. Stringer and McKie give an excellent summary of human migration and its consequences at this time (*African Exodus*, pp. 163–78), and they mention that the ribs of one luckless mammoth in Arizona were found bristling with eight Clovis spearheads. See also Paul Martin, "Prehistoric Overkill: The Global Model," in *Quaternary Extinctions: A Prehistoric Revolution*, eds. Paul S. Martin and Richard G. Klein (Tucson: University of Arizona Press, 1984).

19. Howells, *Mankind in the Making*, p. 206.

20. Tattersall, *Last Neanderthal*, p. 203.

21. Herman Melville, *Moby Dick*, chap. 105. The exact number of bison killed is unknown. Estimates range between 30 million and 60 million. In the 1870s, more than a million a year were being killed by white hunters; by the century's end, only a few hundred animals were left.

22. See, for example, Hugh Brody, *The Other Side of Eden: Hunters, Farmers and the Shaping of the World* (Vancouver: Douglas and McIntyre, 2000).

23. See Crosby, Economic Imperialism, and David Steadman, "Prehistoric Extinctions of Pacific Island Birds," *Science* no. 267 (February 1995): 1123–31.

24. Tim Flannery, *The Future Eaters: An Ecological History of the Australasian Lands and People* (New York: Braziller, 1995).

25. Modern experiments in gathering wild emmer wheat in the Middle East have yielded up to 4,000 pounds an acre (4,500 kilograms a hectare). In Mexico it has been shown that half a day spent reaping *teocintle* (god-corn), a wild relative of maize, will feed a person for ten days (see Ponting, *Green History*, p. 39). Whether *teocintle* (also *teosinte*) is the ancestor of maize or simply a more distant relative is unclear. Some experts believe that domesticated maize, which cannot seed itself without help, crossed with wild relatives and thus killed off its ancestral gene pool — a forewarning of what could happen to other staples if today's genetically modified crops get out of hand.

26. See Tom D. Dillehay, ed., *Monte Verde: A Late Pleistocene Settlement in Chile* (Washington, DC: Smithsonian Books, 1989). For summaries, see Michael E. Moseley, *The Incas and Their Ancestors: The Archaeology of Peru* (London: Thames and Hudson, 1992), pp. 83–85, and Chris Scarre, *Past Worlds: The Times Atlas of Archaeology* (London: Times Books, 1988), p. 70. The remains include medicinal herbs that appear to have been used ritually in a special building.

27. The Australian exception is probably a result of the dry and unreliable climate, and perhaps of a dearth of native plants with crop potential. Australia was populated much earlier than the Americas, and the food crunch — the extinction of big game — may have happened at a time when world climatic instability made agricultural experiments impossible.

28. For example, Jared Diamond's *Guns, Germs, and Steel: The Fates of Human Societies* (New York: W. W. Norton, 1997),

which is informative on germs but should not be relied on for archaeological and historical data or interpretation. In particular, the dating and description of New World agriculture is flawed, and his portrayal of Atahuallpa's overthrow and the other Spanish conquests omits important data and strikes me as tendentious.

29. Quinoa is a non-cereal grain of the *Chenopodium*, or goosefoot, family. New findings from Mexico report domesticated maize by 6,250 years ago (see *Science*, November 14, 2003). High-productivity maize with big cobs was developed about 2,000 years later, when its importance in the diet grew rapidly, and it spread from Mesoamerica to South America. Manioc, a South American plant, went the other way. See Robert J. Sharer, *The Ancient Maya* (Stanford, CA: Stanford University Press, 1994), p. 54.

30. The earliest domesticates in the Andes and Mesoamerica are comparable in age to those of the Middle East. Gathered and cultivated plants dating to 10,000 years ago, including several used for fibre and bedding, have been found at Guitarrero Cave, Peru. The common beans, lima beans, and chiles present were certainly domesticates. Early domestic olluco and potato, also from 10,000 years ago, have been found at Tres Ventanas, in the upper Chilca watershed, and gourds of this age from Ayacucho. See Moseley, *Incas and Their Ancestors*, pp. 96–97.

31. Ancient seeds are much better preserved in dry places than in wet ones, so the importance of lowland areas, such as the jungles of Southeast Asia, New Guinea, and the Amazon, may be underestimated for lack of evidence. New findings from Kuk swamp in New Guinea suggest cultivation of taro, banana, and sugar by 7,000 years ago (see *Science*, July 11, 2003).

32. The painting hangs in the cathedral of Cusco, the old Inca capital. Edward Lanning, in *Peru before the Incas* (Englewood Cliffs, NJ: Prentice-Hall, 1967), gives a good summary of plant and animal domesticates in Peru. The origins and dates of these have since become better known from findings at Guitarrero Cave and elsewhere. Quechua, the Inca language, has a native word for chicken, and there is growing evidence that Peru had chickens of Asian-Polynesian origin before Columbus.

33. Lanning, *Peru before the Incas*, p. 15, lists thirty-nine. See also the National Research Council's *Lost Crops of the Incas* (Washington, DC: National Academy Press, 1989), which lists thirty neglected Andean crops with worldwide potential and describes dozens more from South America. Mesoamerica shared some of these but was equally rich in native plant diversity. Maize and potatoes are about twice as productive as wheat (see Ponting, *Green History*, p. 112). In *Seeds of Change: A Quincentennial Commemoration* (Washington, DC: Smithsonian Institution Press, 1991), Herman Viola and Carolyn Margolis document the impact of New World crops on the Old World, a matter I return to in chapter 5.

34. Stringer and McKie, *African Exodus*, p. 163.

35. Less than two hectares.

36. Four hectares.

37. Thirteen hectares.

38. According to Bruce Trigger (*Early Civilizations*, p. 33): "The main economic factor shaping the development of early civilizations was more intensive food production, in relation to which cutting-tool technologies played only a minor role. . . . The complexity of the tools avail-

able in each early civilization does not correlate with the intensity of agricultural production; nor do any of these civilizations appear to have had tools as elaborate as those possessed by the tribal societies of Iron Age Europe."

39. David Webster, in *The Fall of the Ancient Maya: Solving the Mystery of the Maya Collapse* (London: Thames and Hudson, 2002), p. 77, writes: "Extremely complex societies can evolve in the absence of much technological change, an idea that is very counterintuitive to us because our lives are so affected by rapid and powerful innovations."

40. In China, stone, bronze, and iron "ages" co-existed for a long time, and the technological steps did not follow western Eurasia's supposedly "logical" succession. Bronze was still preferred for weapons long after the discovery of iron. William Watson, in *China* (London: Thames and Hudson, 1961), p. 15, writes: "Iron was cast some centuries before it was forged, thus confounding our Western preconception of the natural development of this technique."

41. Dorothy Hosler, in "Ancient West Mexican Metallurgy: South and Central American Origins and West Mexican Transformations," *American Anthropologist* 90, no. 4 (1988): 832–55, discusses the origin and spread of metallurgical techniques from South America to Mexico, arguing that two distinct metalworking traditions arose in the Andes. Metalworking in the southern Andes has been identified in the form of copper slags at Wankarani sites in Bolivia (the largest of which had over 700 dwellings) and at Waywaka, near Andahuaylas (see Moseley, *Incas and Their Ancestors*, pp. 144, 148). In Inca times, the everyday use of bronze tools became widespread. That some iron, probably meteoric, was known is suggested by the existence of

an old Quechua word for it (*qquillay,* or *kkhellay*). Quipus
(*khipu*) were elaborate records on cords that were stored
in warehouses and tended by a class of public officials.
Meaning was encoded by knot type, position, colour, etc.
The key to reading quipus was lost in the conquest period,
when archives were destroyed and most officials died
or fled. It has been shown that quipu mathematics used
zero (as the Maya did), but on a decimal system, not the
vigesimals of Mesoamerica. Surviving Incas claimed that
quipus could store narrative as well as statistical information. Scholars were sceptical of this until recently, but
new work by Gary Urton suggests that the system was
a "three-dimensional binary code" with at least 1,536
"information units," or signs — more than Sumerian
cuneiform. See *Science,* June 13, 2003.

42. For example, French Meroving skeletons from the early
Middle Ages show chronic starvation, partly because
metal was reserved for weapons, leaving peasants who
no longer knew how to make stone tools scratching the
ground with wooden hoes and ploughs. Georges Duby
and Robert Mandrou quoted in Jane Jacobs, *The Economy
of Cities* (New York: Random House, 1969), pp. 14–15.

43. Çatal Huyük, which is near a volcano, seems to have
traded in obsidian.

44. Gordon Childe, *What Happened in History* (Harmondsworth, UK: Pelican, 1964), p. 74.

45. "Living room" for the German *Volk.*

46. The decline of the Devil since the Enlightenment is illus-
trated by an anecdote from the life of the great French
geologist and naturalist Georges Cuvier (1769–1832). One
of his students dressed up one night as a goatish Devil
and burst into Cuvier's bedroom, threatening to devour

him. Cuvier looked the apparition up and down, and said: "I doubt whether you can. You have horns and hooves. You only eat plants." (Daniel, *The Idea of Prehistory*, p. 34).

47. *The Secret Agent* was published during 1906 as a serial and as a book in 1907. The word "terrorism" arose at the time of the French Revolution, with the sense of mob violence. In 1813, John Adams asked Thomas Jefferson, in a letter recalling the Philadelphia riots, "What think you of Terrorism, Mr. Jefferson?"

48. Some scholars argue that small migrations to the Americas took place from about 50,000 years ago. The accepted mainstream opinion is that people did not settle the Americas until about 15,000 years ago.

49. Australia was a third laboratory. Opinion differs on why farming never developed there (see n. 27, above). There are, however, remains of stone-built villages supported by the regular tending of yams and other wild plants — an important step towards horticulture.

50. These pandemic diseases, and their effect, are discussed in chapter 5.

51. See Richard Alley, *The Two-Mile Time Machine: Ice Cores, Abrupt Climate Change, and Our Future* (Princeton, NJ: Princeton University Press, 2000). By 2004, British researchers had obtained polar ice cores going back 800,000 years (BBC World News, June 9, 2004). One period of severe fluctuations, around 35,000 to 40,000 years ago, may have enabled the southern, warm-weather branch of humanity — the Cro-Magnons — to invade the northern, cold-adapted Neanderthals.

52. Ibid., p. 192. By the end of 2003, world grain reserves had fallen to only 16.2 per cent of consumption, from levels of around 30 per cent between 1990 and 2000. See Martin

Mittelstaedt, "The Larder Is Almost Bare," *Globe and Mail*, May 22, 2004.

53. Mark Lynas, in *High Tide: News from a Warming World* (London: Flamingo, 2004), describes the disappearance of an impressive staircase glacier in Peru. Inge Bolin, in "Our Apus Are Dying!: Glacial Retreat and Its Consequences for Life in the Andes," a paper delivered at the American Anthropological Association meetings in November 2003, reports ethnographic and scientific evidence for the rapid disappearance of others.

III: Fools' Paradise

1. See my definition of civilization in chapter 2. Most archaeologists take 3000 B.C., or thereabouts, as the start of the first full-blown civilizations, Sumer and Egypt. The *rise* towards civilization began about 10,000 years ago, in both the Old and New worlds, with the first steps in plant breeding.
2. Quoted in Daniel, *The Idea of Prehistory*, pp. 14–15.
3. Letter of Francisco de Toledo, March 25, 1571, quoted in Luis A. Pardo, ed., *Saqsaywaman* no. 1 (July 1970): 144.
4. From *The Journal of Jacob Roggeveen*, trans. and ed. Andrew Sharp (Oxford: Clarendon Press, 1970). Quoted in Paul Bahn and John Flenley, *Easter Island, Earth Island* (London: Thames and Hudson, 1992), p. 13, and more fully in Catherine and Michel Orliac, *Easter Island*, trans. Paul G. Bahn, (New York: Harry N. Abrams, 1995), pp. 98–99.
5. Orliac, *Easter Island*, p. 17.
6. Both land and sea were, however, less rich in species than large tropical archipelagoes such as Fiji and the Tahitian islands. Like the Marquesas, Easter Island lacks a surrounding coral reef.
7. Or an extinct species closely related to the Chilean palm.

8. Most of these were ultimately of Southeast Asian origin. The sweet potato was indeed from South America and is known throughout Polynesia (*pace* Bahn and Flenley, *Easter Island*) by versions of its Quechua name, *kumara*. For reasons unknown, the pig did not make the voyage.

9. In their otherwise excellent book on Easter Island, Bahn and Flenley (ibid., p. 46) are wrong in stating that the ancient Peruvians lacked ships with sails. There was a sophisticated sailing culture, using ocean-going *balsas*, along the South American coast since Tiwanaku times (the first millennium A.D.). In Inca times, such craft made regular trading voyages up the coast of the empire from Chincha, and other ports south of Lima, to Guayaquil and from there to Panama. The ships were similar to the *Kon-Tiki* design but larger and more sophisticated. Equipped with multiple centreboards, they could tack against the wind and were still making round trips to the Galapagos in the eighteenth century — 600 miles (almost 1,000 kilometres) each way. Pizarro learnt of the Inca Empire in 1526 by intercepting a trading fleet heading for Panama from their home port of Tumbez. The craft he boarded had a twenty-man crew and was carrying thirty tons of freight. The Spaniards compared it, in its size and sailing gear, to their own caravels. It is also known that pre-Inca Peruvian seafarers reached the Galapagos on several occasions, leaving behind distinctive pottery. It is just possible that pre-Inca Peruvians reached the Marquesas, which may have been the migration "hub" for Easter Island, Hawaii, and other island groups. I think it equally possible that Polynesian canoes occasionally reached the South American coast and returned to their home islands. Spanish chroniclers recorded accounts of a fifteenth-

century expedition by Tupa Inca Yupanqui (Atahuallpa's grandfather) to inhabited islands two months' sailing from Peru — see Thor Heyerdahl, *Sea Routes to Polynesia* (London: Allen and Unwin, 1968), chap. 4 and 5, for a review of this evidence and its influence on early Spanish explorations. It seems unlikely that an Inca ruler would personally sail away from his empire for a year, but he may have commissioned such an expedition.

10. 166 square kilometres.
11. Bahn and Flenley, *Easter Island*, p. 214.
12. Nine metres.
13. Twenty metres.
14. James Cook, quoted in ibid., p. 170.
15. Ibid., p. 165.
16. In general this was avoided, though not at Coventry and Dresden.
17. Roggeveen killed at least a dozen. Attacks by foreigners later became systematic, as "blackbirding," the enslavement of Polynesians, took hold throughout the Pacific. In 1805, the American ship *Nancy* killed many islanders while kidnapping others for forced labour. In 1822, the whaler *Pindos* seized young girls to "amuse" her crew, flinging them overboard when the sailors had had enough. But the worst came in 1862, when Peruvian slave raiders took away half or more of the population to the "islands of death," the infamous British-financed guano diggings off the Peruvian coast, where labourers were chained together and worked until they dropped. Only fifteen made it back alive to Easter Island (after humanitarian appeals by the bishop of Tahiti), and they brought smallpox with them. By 1872, when Pierre Loti saw it, the island was a mass grave, with scarcely more than a

hundred people left alive (Bahn and Flenley, *Easter Island*, p. 179).

18. Those standing today have been restored.

19. Bahn and Flenley, *Easter Island*, pp. 213, 218.

20. The island even had a form of script, called *rongorongo*, though many experts believe it to be post-contact in origin.

21. Sumer and Egypt about 3000 B.C.; the Indus Valley about 2500 B.C.; Shang China by 1700 B.C.; Minoan Crete and Mycenaean Greece by 1700 and 1500 B.C., respectively; Olmec Mexico and Chavín Peru by 1200 B.C. Important new work on the Peruvian coast has shown irrigation and urbanism (including pyramids totalling 2 million cubic metres) beginning at Caral about 2600 B.C.

22. Mesopotamia, India, Egypt, and Greece shared the same Fertile Crescent grains. China, Mexico, and Peru developed their own crops, sharing others later. The degree that cultural features such as art, mathematics, and writing diffused within the two hemispheres is hotly debated by rival schools of thought. In my view, early Chinese civilization was almost as independent from others as the civilizations of Mexico and Peru.

23. These include Assyrians, Babylonians, Phoenicians, Jews, Arabs, and all other speakers of Semitic languages.

24. N. K. Sandars, trans., *The Epic of Gilgamesh* (Harmondsworth, UK: Penguin, 1972), p. 65. Few of these texts exist in the original Sumerian language; most of them have come down in Assyrian or Babylonian rescensions. Sandars therefore uses the later Semitic names of characters and deities. The Sumerian original of the goddess Ishtar, for example, was Inanna. Anu, the god of heaven and father of other gods, was An; Shamash the Sun was Utu; and Ea, the god of wisdom, was Enki.

25. Four hectares and twelve hectares, respectively.
26. Marshall Sahlins has called hunter-gathering the "origi-
    nal affluent society" because fewer hours of work were
    needed for food and shelter (Sahlins, *Stone Age Economics*
    [London: Tavistock Publications, 1972], chap. 1). The life-
    expectancy figures for Çatal Hüyük (Scarre, *Past Worlds*,
    p. 82) are not bad by ancient standards, but they are proba-
    bly lower than among most hunter-gatherer groups. Figures
    are deduced from the many burials within the houses.
27. See Charles Redman, *Human Impact on Ancient Environments*
    (Tucson: University of Arizona Press, 1999), pp. 106–109.
    Evidence includes pollen, charcoal, layers of ash and sedi-
    ment. Work by Gary and Ilse Rollefson at Ain Ghazal, in
    Jordan, has provided key evidence of environmental degra-
    dation. Houses got smaller as timber thicknesses decreased,
    while game became scarcer and less varied.
28. By the 1970s, the largest stand of cedars left in Lebanon
    had only 400 trees. W. B. Fisher, *The Middle East: A Physi-
    cal, Social and Regional Geography* (London: Methuen, 1978),
    p. 95.
29. Gordon Childe, *New Light on the Most Ancient East* (Lon-
    don: Routledge and Kegan Paul, 1954), p. 114. This work
    was first published, as *The Most Ancient East*, in 1928.
30. This is the famous and still controversial "hydraulic the-
    ory" for the origins of civilization, advanced by Julian
    Steward in 1949. While not applicable to every civiliza-
    tion, it still has merit in the cases of Mesopotamia, Egypt,
    and the Indus valley.
31. See Trigger, *Early Civilizations*, p. 9, citing Robert McCor-
    mick Adams, *Heartland of Cities: Surveys of Ancient
    Settlement and Land Use on the Central Floodplain of the
    Euphrates* (Chicago: University of Chicago Press, 1981).

32. These were built of mud brick, with a more weatherproof facing of plaster, coloured tiles, or stone and burnt brick; the top and stages were surfaced with tar, the earliest known use of Iraqi oil. In its height and its use of coloured tile in geometric patterns, the ziggurat was a forerunner of the minaret.

33. Childe, *What Happened in History*, p. 101.

34. In places where good stone such as flint and obsidian is abundant, the advantages of bronze do not necessarily outweigh the cost and effort of working it. But where all raw materials are imported from afar, bronze tools have the advantage of being endlessly reparable: a broken axe or blade can be recast or made into something else. Broken stone tools, by contrast, are mostly rubbish.

35. Sacred sex and prostitution are found in many cultures. The Sumerian "harlots" were probably similar to the temple hetaerae of Classical Greece. This Mesopotamian custom doubtless contributed to the later biblical view of Babylon as the "Great Whore."

36. See, for example, the apocryphal story "Bel and the Dragon," in which Daniel shows the king of Babylon how his priests are deceiving him.

37. 450 hectares.

38. Ur was only 150 acres (sixty hectares), a more typical Sumerian size. Populations probably ranged between 50,000 for Uruk and 10,000 to 20,000 for Ur and the rest — comparable to many mid-sized early cities in both hemispheres, and to those of mediaeval Europe, but far short of Rome, which had about half a million people, or Tenochtitlan (Mexico City) with about a quarter-million. See chapter 4, note 20, below.

39. Sandars, *Gilgamesh*, p. 61.

40. M. E. L. Mallowan, in *Early Mesopotamia and Iran* (London: Thames and Hudson, 1965), cites textual evidence from Lagash of the first "separation between church and state" (p. 88).

41. Enduring among Europeans until the French Revolution and among the Japanese until 1945.

42. Ponting, *Green History*, p. 58.

43. J. M. Coetzee, *Waiting for the Barbarians* (London: Penguin, 1982), p. 79.

44. This tomb is from the Early Dynastic period, level II or III, not to be confused with the post-Sargonid Third Dynasty of Ur.

45. In early China, a Shang tomb held 165 human sacrifices (see Scarre, *Past Worlds*, p. 147, and Watson, *China*, p. 69).

46. Cahokia's largest pyramid, which covers sixteen acres (six and a half hectares) at the base and rises 100 feet (thirty metres), is one of the world's biggest buildings of any period, and the largest in the United States before the twentieth century. The city centre had an enclosed precinct of 300 acres (120 hectares), and the total urban centre was at least 1,200 acres (490 hectares). See Scarre, *Past Worlds*, pp. 230–31; Jack Weatherford, *Native Roots: How the Indians Enriched America* (New York: Crown, 1991), pp. 6–18; Joseph A. Tainter, *The Collapse of Complex Societies* (Cambridge: Cambridge University Press, 1988), p. 16; Carl Waldman, *Atlas of the North American Indian* (New York: Facts on File, 1985), p. 22; Melvin Fowler, "A Pre-Columbian Urban Center on the Mississippi," *Scientific American*, August 1975. Estimates of Cahokia's population range from 20,000 to 75,000; from the large area it occupied and the number of mounds (about 120), I doubt the city had fewer than 40,000 people in its thirteenth-century

heyday. The related Natchez people further south continued the practice of servant burial into historic times.

47. Quoted in Nancy Jay, *Throughout Your Generations Forever: Sacrifice, Religion, and Paternity* (Chicago: University of Chicago Press, 1992).

48. The legend of Adam and Eve has its flaws (not the least being the source of their sons' wives), but it contains a humanitarian message: that all human beings are kin. As the renegade priest John Ball put it in a fourteenth-century rap rhyme during England's Peasant Revolt: "When Adam delved and Eve span / Who was then a gentleman?" Ball, an excommunicated priest who recommended killing all lords and lawyers (see Shakespeare's *Henry VI, Part Two*), was himself killed by Richard II in 1381.

49. Several Inca kings — including, for example, Manku Qhapaq and Wayna Qhapaq (also spelled as Manco Capac and Huayna Capac) — had this word in their names. In modern Quechua, *qhapaq* simply means rich.

50. Quoted in Sahlins, *Stone Age Economics*, p. 259.

51. China has had a famine in at least one province nearly every year of the past 2,000 (Ponting, *Green History*, p. 103).

52. 130 kilometres.

53. Basra, like Baghdad, was built by Muslim invaders in the seventh century A.D.; it was taken and occupied by British forces in 2003.

54. 320 kilometres.

55. Or floods. Archaeologists have found evidence of several catastrophic inundations in the earliest Sumerian levels.

56. Utnapishtim was from the city of Shurrupak, the modern Fara, one of the first to gain prominence (see Sandars, *Gil-*

gamesh, p. 40). This suggests that the great flood(s) behind
the legend happened early in Sumerian times, when the
cities were more easily swamped. Utnapishtim's name
means "the Faraway"; after the flood, he becomes a water
spirit at the edge of the Persian Gulf.

57. These excerpts are from Sandars's translation, pp. 108–13.

58. Quoted in Ponting, *Green History*, p. 70.

59. The flood stories may reflect some awareness of the human
load on nature. Enlil is provoked to destroy mankind
because of human noise and numbers, and after the flood,
human fertility and lifespan were reduced.

60. Tainter, *Complex Societies*, p. 7.

61. Quoted in Ponting, *Green History*. I have relied mainly on
Ponting's excellent summary (pp. 68–73) and that of Redman (*Human Impact*, pp. 133–39).

62. From the Food and Agriculture Organization (FAO) statistics charted in Goudie, *Natural Environment*, p. 170.
The figure for Iraq does not include lands no longer in
use. Fisher (*Middle East*, p. 85) estimates that 80 per cent
of Iraq's cropland is saline "to some extent," and that
one per cent becomes "unusable" each year. Egypt is also
getting salty, but much of its problem is recent, following
the building of the Aswan High Dam in the 1950s, which
reduced watering and flushing of the Nile valley, trading Egypt's natural ecology for an artificial one more like
Iraq's.

IV: Pyramid Schemes

1. See chapter 1 and Pollard, *Idea of Progress*.

2. Adams estimated half a million for Sumer, which Trigger (*Early Civilizations*, p. 30) accepts. This may be on the
cautious side, but given the known size of the cities, and

the fact that most people lived within them, the total is unlikely to have been more than twice that. Estimates for the Maya in the eighth century A.D. vary widely but cluster in the 5-million range for the lowlands, to which we might add a million or two for highland Guatemala and Chiapas. Webster, who generally errs on the low side, cites geographical studies suggesting about 3 million for some 9,000 square miles (23,000 square kilometres) of the heartland, only a tenth of the whole Maya area. He arrives at a lowland total of 4 to 5 million, but feels this may still be too high (Webster, *Ancient Maya*, pp. 173–74). Linda Schele and David Freidel, in *A Forest of Kings: The Untold Story of the Ancient Maya* (New York: Morrow, 1990), pp. 57–59, accept the estimate of half a million for the Tikal kingdom alone; the other states, of which there may have been as many as sixty by the eighth century, were below 50,000 each.

3. Despite Sumer's great influence on later civilizations, the Sumerian ethnic identity died out. The language survived only as a dead tongue revered by Babylonian scholars, with no living relatives.

4. There are more than twenty related but distinct Mayan languages, each one roughly corresponding to the territory of an ancient city-state. Native speakers of Mayan are increasingly involved in the decipherment of pre-Columbian texts, and Maya calendar-priests, or "daykeepers," have kept parts of the calendar alive since ancient times. Maya political activists include Rigoberta Menchú, winner of the 1992 Nobel Peace Prize. See W. George Lovell, *Conquest and Survival in Colonial Guatemala: A Historical Geography of the Cuchumatán Highlands 1500–1821*, 2nd ed. (Montreal: McGill-Queen's University

Press, 1992), and *A Beauty That Hurts: Life and Death in Guatemala* (Austin: University of Texas Press, 2000); Rigoberta Menchú, *I, Rigoberta Menchú: An Indian Woman in Guatemala*, trans. Ann Wright (London: Verso, 1984); and Barbara Tedlock, *Time and the Highland Maya* (Albuquerque: University of New Mexico Press, 1982).

5. Ronald Wright, *A Scientific Romance* (London: Anchor, 1997), pp. 66, 259; Ronald Wright, "Civilization Is a Pyramid Scheme," *Globe and Mail*, August 5, 2000.

6. Edward Gibbon, *The History of the Decline and Fall of the Roman Empire* (London: Folio Society, 1995), p. 31.

7. The term "neo-Europe" for the United States, Australia, Argentina, etc., was coined by Alfred Crosby (*Ecological Imperialism*, pp. 2–3). I refer here to the imperial expansion of the United States across her continent in the nineteenth century. American national mythology sees this as "pioneering" and "settlement," but the conquest and dispossession of one Indian people after another, including organized native states such as the Cherokee and Iroquois, was clearly imperial, a forerunner in deed if not in name of Germany's *Lebensraum*. The U.S. historian Patricia Nelson Limerick writes: "There is no clearer fact in American history than the fact of conquest. In North America, just as in South America . . . Europeans invaded a land fully occupied by natives." Patricia Nelson Limerick, *Something in the Soil* (New York: Norton, 2000), p. 33.

8. It is often forgotten that Classical sculpture was originally painted in bright colours and adorned with bits of clothing, metal, and hair, not unlike mediaeval religious images.

9. One of the worst features of the goat is that it can climb up into lower branches, killing even mature trees by gnawing

off the bark. W. B. Fisher (*Middle East*, p. 91) writes: "Unrestricted grazing, particularly by 'sharp poisoned tooth of the goat,' is one of the fundamental causes of agricultural backwardness in the Middle East." Sheep can also be a problem, especially when introduced outside their natural range, where native plants may not be able to withstand them.

10. I have seen fields in Peru so steep that farmers sometimes literally fall out of them.

11. See Ponting, *Green History*, p. 76.

12. Quoted in ibid., pp. 76–77; see also Richard Manning, "The Oil We Eat," *Harper's Magazine*, February 2004, pp. 37–45. *Critias* can be read online at classics.mit.edu, in a different translation by Benjamin Jowett.

13. From *Amores*, Book 3. trans. Guy Lee (London: John Murray, 1968), republished in 2000 as *Ovid in Love*.

14. The town was Salamis.

15. Tainter, *Complex Societies*, p. 132.

16. John Milton, *Paradise Lost*, book 4. The younger William Pitt, speaking in the House of Commons on November 18, 1783, added that it was also "the creed of slaves."

17. Trigger, *Early Civilizations*, pp. 8–9.

18. The period from 27 B.C. to A.D. 284 is known to historians as the principate; it was followed by the dominate. Not until Diocletian would emperors become formal monarchs, with all the panoply of Oriental despots.

19. The "hawks" saw no reason why Rome shouldn't do even better, following the silk road to its source near the ocean on the far side of the world.

20. Estimates for Rome range from 400,000 to one million, though it is not clear how much of the surrounding city-state is included in these. Even though most Romans

lived in crowded tenements, the five square miles (dozen square kilometres) within the Aurelian walls can't have housed more than a few hundred thousand, especially given the many squares and public buildings. It is possible that greater Rome, including the outlying suburbs, barracks, and villas, approached a million at its height. Other cities in the Roman Empire were much smaller, except Constantinople, with its population of 200,000 to 400,000 in the fourth century A.D., and Antioch in Syria. Teotihuacan, a Mexican grid city that covered eight square miles (twenty-one square kilometres), is thought to have had about 250,000 people in its heyday, between the first and seventh centuries A.D. Early Chinese cities were built mainly of wood and earth, so little survives on which to base estimates; however, by late Chou times (the third and fourth centuries B.C.), the city of G'a-to covered some twelve square miles (thirty-one square kilometres) and may have held 270,000 (see Paul Wheatley, *The Pivot of the Four Quarters: A Preliminary Enquiry into the Origins and Character of the Ancient Chinese City* [Edinburgh: Edinburgh University Press, 1971], p. 183). Urbanism did not rise sharply in China until the eleventh century A.D., when the population of a number of cities reached several hundred thousand.

21. Webster, *Ancient Maya*, p. 150; Goudie, *Natural Environment*, p. 32.

22. The city of Mexico, comprising the twin cities of Tenochtitlan and Tlatelolco, was built on artificially extended islands in a large lake that has since been drained. It had public latrines and employed a thousand street sweepers. Sewage was taken out by canoe for use on fields. Cortés himself wrote that the main square was so great

that a town of 500 could easily be built inside it, and that there were forty "towers" (pyramids), the largest of which was "higher than that of the cathedral of Seville" (quoted in Viola and Margolis, *Seeds of Change*, pp. 36–37). The city had about a quarter-million residents in 1519, and no more than that until the late nineteenth century. Moshe Safdie, in *The City After the Automobile: An Architect's Vision* (Toronto: Stoddart, 1997), p. 85, notes Mexico City's extraordinary modern growth, from 345,000 in 1900 to more than 21 million in the 1990s.

23. See chapters 2 and 3.

24. See Dickens's description of "Coketown" in *Hard Times*, quoted in chapter 5, note 39, below.

25. Tainter, *Complex Societies*, p. 143. In this case, the silver coins were Egyptian drachmae, pegged with the denarius and equally debased. Fisher (*Middle East*, p. 160), following Pliny, notes that as Roman trade with the Far East for silk and other Oriental luxuries grew, "between one-quarter and one-half" of the empire's gold and silver flowed to Asia.

26. Tainter, *Complex Societies*, p. 147. In 378, for example, Balkan miners defected to the Visigoths.

27. In the Biferno region, the impact was "unparalleled in the valley's history until modern times" (Redman, *Human Impact*, p. 116). The Vera basin of southeastern Spain shows the same: population (and erosion) rising steeply, then collapsing by A.D. 400. This valley had also undergone an earlier cycle of destruction caused by intensive barley farming in the Bronze Age; this was followed by a thousand years of abandonment until early Roman times.

28. Nine metres.

29. Ponting, *Green History*, pp. 77–78.

30. Just over one square kilometre.
31. See the Old English poem "The Ruin" from the *Exeter Book*.
32. Ten hectares.
33. If the world then held 200 million, I think it likely that the Americas had 30 to 50 million, as did China and India each. Ponting's estimates of only 5 million for all of the New World in A.D. 200 and 14 million in 1300 are far too low (Ponting, *Green History*, pp. 92–93). Most experts now accept a New World total of 80 to 100 million in 1492, when the world total was 350 to 400 million.
34. The First, or Chavín, Horizon is named after a temple-city in the central Andes called Chavín de Huantar. Some experts view its ornately carved stone ruins as a pilgrimage centre; others think it was a political capital.
35. Nearly 4,000 metres.
36. Tiwanaku (or Tiahuanaco) had 30,000 to 60,000 people. The capital of an empire eventually ruined by drought, Tiwanaku left behind canals, raised fields, and megalithic buildings whose virtuoso stonework impressed the Incas a thousand years later. Its relationship with Wari (Huari), a city near modern Ayacucho, is still unclear; although they shared an art style and some iconography, they may have been rival states. See Alan Kolata, *Tiwanaku and Its Hinterland: Archaeology and Paleoecology of an Andean Civilization* (Washington, DC: Smithsonian Books, 1996); and Charles Stanish, *Ancient Titicaca: The Evolution of Complex Society in Southern Peru and Northern Bolivia* (Berkeley, CA: University of California Press, 2003).
37. Twenty-one square kilometres.
38. The white man was not the first to be guilty of urban sprawl in great rectangles across American landscapes.
39. Webster, for example, (*Ancient Maya*, p. 297) notes maize

pollen at Copan by 2000 B.C. Other Maya cities also began as farming villages at about this time.

40. The early text is on a stela at El Portón, in highland Guatemala. See Sharer, *Ancient Maya*, p. 79.

41. Nine hectares.

42. This is the Danta platform at El Mirador, which measures 1,000 feet (300 metres) on each side and is 230 feet (70 metres) tall. Some of its volume is a natural hillock, but other buildings of comparable size are known from this time. The El Tigre complex has a base six times larger than that of the biggest Classic temple at Tikal. Ibid., p. 114ff.

43. Sixty metres.

44. In the Old World, the Babylonians came closest to a positional number system, but seem to have lacked a true zero. Some experts now believe that the late Babylonians did develop a true zero around 300 B.C., when the Seleucid dynasty was installed by Alexander. If this is so, the Hindu zero could have been derived from Babylonia. It has long been accepted that the modern "Arabic" system first appeared in northern India in the sixth century A.D., and reached Baghdad from India in the eighth century. European mathematicians began to see the system's advantages in the twelfth century, but full adoption took centuries more. The Olmec and the Maya probably perfected their system in the sixth century B.C., more than a thousand years before the Hindus (and two or three centuries before Seleucid Babylon). Curiously, though the Maya system is vigesimal (based on twenties), Maya languages imply a decimal count: the word "thirteen" (*oxlahun*) is formed from the words for "three" (*ox*) and "ten" (*lahun*), as in English and most other languages.

The Incas of South America also had zero, with a decimal place system, but its date of origin is unknown. Some scholars who believe in trans-Pacific contacts suggest that Asian arithmetic may have been influenced by the Americas — controversial but not impossible, especially given the extreme rarity of the invention of zero.

45. Egyptian writing is quite unlike Sumerian, but the *idea* of writing may have been derived from Sumer. The same may be true of the Indus valley script, which is still undeciphered. An interesting and well-documented case of writing being stimulated but not copied is that of the Cherokee syllabics invented by Sequoyah in the early nineteenth century. See Michael D. Coe, *Breaking the Maya Code* (London: Thames and Hudson, 1992), for the story of Maya decipherment.

46. Trigger (*Early Civilizations*, p. 8ff) notes that civilizations that invented writing wholly on their own did so early in their careers.

47. See Sharer, *Ancient Maya*, for a good summary of Maya astronomy, and Ronald Wright, *Time Among the Maya* (London: Bodley Head, 1989), for a description of the calendar's workings and examples of some extraordinarily remote calculations. Eric Thompson, *Maya Hieroglyphic Writing* (Norman: University of Oklahoma Press, 1971), and David H. Kelley, *Deciphering the Maya Script* (Austin: University of Texas, 1976), are still among the best resources on the calendar, though their work on the writing is now dated.

48. Sharer, *Ancient Maya*, p. 471.

49. See ibid., pp. 467–76. Most Maya cities, unlike those of Mexico, were not laid out on grids; the urban area faded gradually into the surrounding country. The "limits" of

Tikal are earthworks and basins that enclose about fifty square miles (120 square kilometres) of core settlement. Some Mayanists argue for a system of many city-states, nominally independent, though arranged in a shifting power hierarchy rather like modern nation-states. Others believe that some of the greater cities established short-lived empires, as Athens did in Greece.

50. 200 per square kilometre.

51. See ibid., p. 471, and T. Patrick Culbert and Don S. Rice, .eds., *Precolumbian Population History in the Maya Lowlands* (Albuquerque: University of New Mexico Press, 1990). See also Webster, *Ancient Maya*, pp. 173–74, for an overview of the population question. However, I think he underestimates the extent of intensive farming, and his description of Maya cities as merely "royal centres" seems to revive the long-discredited ceremonial-centre model. In other respects, his book is the best and most up-to-date summary of the Maya collapse available.

52. The Aztecs, who had a similar system in the shallow lakes around Mexico City, were raising up to four crops a year. In hill country, the Maya sometimes built terraces to hold the earth, but not on the scale of Asia or the Andes. Residents of the city of Tiwanaku, up in the Bolivian Andes, also built raised fields around Lake Titicaca, though only potatoes and other high-altitude crops such as olluco and quinoa would grow there. In this case, the canals acted as heat sinks, warding off frost; their restoration in some areas has brought a big increase in yields. Trigger (*Early Civilizations*, pp. 28–34) outlines Aztec and other ancient modes of food production.

53. Huxley's *Beyond the Mexique Bay* is eccentric and now very

dated on Maya archaeology, but it's still an interesting book on the region in the 1930s.

54. Impressive replicas of Maya buildings were on show at the 1893 Chicago World's Fair. See Barbara Braun, *Pre-Columbian Art and the Post-Columbian World: Ancient American Sources of Modern Art* (New York: Abrams, 1993), for a fascinating survey of the pre-Columbian influence on modern art and architecture.

55. These buildings all went up in the 115 years between Tikal's victory over its archrival, Calakmul, in 695 and the completion of Temple III in or before 810. (See Webster, *Ancient Maya*, chap. 8.) All seem to have been designed as royal tombs, a kingly appropriation of public space, a new thing in Mesoamerica. Kings and nobility had previously been buried in existing temple platforms. The most impressive crypt is Pacal's tomb at Palenque, found complete with a slaughtered retinue along the corridors and stairs.

56. Or sometime between 790 and 792. These dates are poorly preserved.

57. Except for a quixotic flicker in 869.

58. Some experts still dispute the correlation between the Long Count calendar and ours, but most accept the Goodman-Martinez-Thompson correlation in one of two versions that vary by only two days. Though the post-Classic Maya dropped the Long Count, they did remember it, and a related calendar called the Short Count continued to be used into Spanish times. Parts of this system are still kept by daykeepers in Guatemala to this day. Recently, these calendar-priests have themselves revived the use of the Long Count, and are printing almanacs.

59. Webster, *Ancient Maya*, pp. 273–74.
60. Ibid., p. 312.
61. Ibid., p. 317.
62. Ibid., p. 309.
63. If drought was the main cause, one would expect Yucatán, which is dry at the best of times, to have suffered
the most. Average rainfall at Mérida is thirty-seven
inches (ninety-four centimetres), about half that at Tikal
(ibid., p. 244). Most of Yucatán has no rivers or lakes,
only underground water in natural cenotes (from Maya
dzonot) and man-made cisterns. Anxiety over rainfall
was always high; many of Yucatán's ancient buildings
are covered in sculpted faces of Chac, the god of rain
and water. But the Maya fell hardest in their heartland,
the Peten jungle. In Yucatán to the north and the highlands to the south, the civilization continued, building
towns and transcribing its old knowledge well into
Spanish times. Some Yucatec Maya could still read and
write the ancient script until the beginning of the eighteenth century. It is also true that a few Maya towns did
survive in the jungle: notably Tayasal, on Lake Peten
Itza, and Lamanai and Tipu, in Belize. But these were
modest affairs. I doubt that the jungle's population had
recovered to even a tenth of its Classic levels when the
Spaniards arrived. After that, European and African
diseases ruled out any significant recovery before Victorian times. However, until Tayasal's conquest in 1697,
its numbers were swollen from time to time by refugees
from Spanish territory.
64. Maya civilization seems to have stumbled twice before: at
the end of the pre-Classic (about A.D. 200) and again in
the mid-Classic (the sixth century). Severe drought may

well have been a factor, causing wars and upheaval but not general collapse.

65. The Black Death of the mid-fourteenth century relieved land pressure in Europe, while the resulting labour short-age spurred innovation and social mobility. The recovery of the Maya was interrupted by smallpox and other new plagues brought by the Spaniards.

66. The Biferno valley, severely eroded during Roman times, does not show another period of intense exploitation and erosion until the fifteenth century (Redman, *Human Impact*, p. 116). At the Maya city of Copan, pollen studies show the forest beginning to return about A.D. 1250; Web-ster (*Ancient Maya*, pp. 312–14) describes the stratigraphy of modern cornfields among the ruins. Renewed farming in this area and in the jungle is mainly recent — little was seen by explorers such as John L. Stephens and Frederick Catherwood in the mid-nineteenth century. Roman North Africa, as noted before, has not recovered and is now largely desert.

67. The hills had been wooded for a while after the Ice Age ended, but were largely desert by the time Egyptian civili-zation began.

68. 39,000 square kilometres.

69. In 3,000 years, the only major innovations were the intro-duction of *shadduf* (bucket-and-pole) irrigation about 1300 B.C. and the *sagiya* waterwheel about 300 B.C. Stone tools, such as flint sickles and knives, were still widespread in Middle Kingdom times.

70. Egypt's ecology has changed greatly since the building of the Aswan High Dam in the 1950s. The bulk of the silt no longer reaches the fields, and it has been replaced by manure and chemical fertilizer; salinization and waterlog-

ging are becoming very serious problems. J. A. Wilson, in "Egypt through the New Kingdom: Civilization without Cities," in *City Invincible*, eds. C. H. Kraeling and Robert McCormick Adams (Chicago: University of Chicago Press, 1960), called Egypt "the civilization without cities" because most of its people lived in small villages on dry ground behind the riverside fields.

71. From 3000 B.C. until A.D. 1500, the world's average growth rate was nearly 0.1 per cent (Ponting, *Green History*, pp. 89–90), doubling the population about every 800 years. Egypt's Old Kingdom is thought to have had between 1.2 and 2 million people; the Middle Kingdom between 2 and 3 million. There was probably a peak of 6 or 7 million at the start of the Ptolemaic period, but this fell somewhat by Roman times. As recently as 1882, the total was still only 6.7 million, showing no overall gain in the more than 2,000 years since the pharaohs (Alfred Crosby, *The Columbian Exchange: Biological and Cultural Consequences of 1492* [Westport, CN: Greenwood Press, 1972], p. 190). By 1964, it had risen to 28.9 million; Crosby attributes much of this rise to the introduction of maize. Since 1964, the population has doubled again, but Egyptians now are eating mainly imported wheat and feeding their maize to livestock (see Timothy Mitchell, "The Object of Development: America's Egypt," in Jonathan Crush, ed., *The Power of Development* [London: Routledge, 1995]).

72. 150 per square kilometre.

73. Studies of Egyptian mummies show poor health even among the upper classes. Parasitic infections spread by crowded living and unsafe water were common, and the heavily exploited lower classes were also malnourished.

74. The main crop was millet, until wheat appeared around

1300 B.C. It took wheat 6,000 years to reach China after its domestication on the far side of the continent, hardly the rapid transit of technology in the Old World argued by Diamond (*Guns, Germs, and Steel*).

75. The main trade item was silk, which flowed indirectly from China to Rome along the Silk Road. The two empires had only hazy ideas of each other's existence.

76. Chinese records show nearly one famine every year in at least one province from 108 B.C. to 1910 (Ponting, *Green History*, p. 105).

V: The Rebellion of the Tools

1. Tainter, *Complex Societies*, p. 59.

2. Europe, North Africa, and other parts of the Old World lost about a third of their population in the Black Death of the mid-fourteenth century. In Europe, this broke down old hierarchies and encouraged the use of mills and other simple machinery. In the Islamic world, the heavy loss of workers damaged irrigation works and caused economic decline, contributing to the Christian *reconquista* of Spain. In 1500, European pandemics had not yet struck the New World population, which probably numbered 80 to 100 million — between a fifth and a quarter of world total. By 1600, in densely populated regions such as Mesoamerica, the Andes, and the North American Southeast, population levels had fallen by more than 90 per cent. An overall loss of at least 50 million for the New World during the sixteenth century is a cautious guess; losses could have been as high as 75 million or even more, depending on the initial figure.

3. The world's population currently grows at just over 70 million a year, down from 90 million a year in the 1980s.

4. Redman, *Human Impact*, p. 124. For example, the Colca valley (*qollqa* means "granary") was almost wholly terraced by Inca times, and terraces still in use can also be seen along the Urubamba valley, near Cusco. The guano was mined by seafaring Chincha merchants and packed up into the mountains by llama train on paved roads. Inca use of guano would have been sustainable indefinitely if it didn't outpace the deposition rate of pelican droppings. Like Egypt and China, Peru had a subsidy from nature. The deposits were rediscovered and mined out in the infamous "guano boom" of mid-Victorian times. See also note 25, below.

5. The name means, roughly, "the United Four Quarters."

6. Almost 5,000 kilometres.

7. The Aztec Empire may have had somewhat more than the Inca Empire, which was far bigger but less urbanized. Estimates range from 6 to 32 million for the Incas and 12 to 25 million for the Aztecs, with the higher figures gaining acceptance. Whatever the true figures were, it is safe to assume that Mesoamerica (which included the Maya and other peoples beyond Aztec control) and Tawantinsuyu (the Inca Empire) together held at least half the population of the New World. For a dated but still useful discussion of world population estimates and sources, see Fernand Braudel, "Weight of Numbers," in *The Structures of Everyday Life* (New York: Harper and Row, 1981).

8. 22,500 kilometres.

9. The command economy functioned mainly at the imperial level. Local peoples seem to have run their own affairs, within limits. The Chincha, for example, played an important role as seafaring merchants, trading luxury goods with Panama and possibly western Mexico. Early Spanish and

native sources confirm that the basic needs of life — food, shelter, clothing — were met by the Inca state in times of want. Evidently, food production matched demand, even though population was high for the Andean region's harsh and diverse environment. Nostalgia for a golden age known as "the time of the Inca" became a unifying feature of revolts against Spain for three centuries. Rebel leaders, including one in seventeenth-century Argentina who was Spanish-born, took Inca names and titles. See Luis Millones, "The Time of the Inca: The Colonial Indians' Quest," *Antiquity* no. 66 (1992): 204–16. The greatest Indian uprising, the 1780 revolt of Inca Tupa Amaru II, who was a genuine descendant of Inca royalty, came close to expelling Spain from Peru — only forty years before *criollo* (white-settler) revolts created the Latin American republics. In Mexico there were no comparable efforts to reinstate Aztec rule, though elements of the pre-Columbian world did inspire Mexican nationalism.

10. Geoffrey W. Conrad and Arthur A. Demarest, in *Religion and Empire* (Cambridge: Cambridge University Press, 1984), argue that the political dynamics of their expansion made them inherently unstable. This may be true, though I think no more so than of other empires at a comparable stage (Rome in the time of Julius Caesar, for example). The Aztec hegemony, being highly exploitive and widely hated, was probably the shakier of the two. There is also evidence that both were trying to reform themselves to achieve long-term stability. It is important to remember that the civil wars and disintegration that Pizarro found in Peru were wholly a result of smallpox and other Old World plagues.

11. Smallpox typically kills 50 to 75 per cent in a "virgin soil"

pandemic. A Maya chronicle gives a snapshot of the plague's initial effect on the royal family of one kingdom: of four Cakchiquel rulers mentioned by name, three died at the same time. Huayna Capac of Peru (Atahuallpa's father) and his designated heir died, as did Cuitlahuac, who had taken over in Mexico after Moctezuma was killed. All these pandemics are thought to have developed from the interaction of humans and domestic animals in the Old World, especially Asia. New World farming relied more heavily on plants; and the American animals that were domesticated do not seem to have harboured disease transmissible to humans.

12. Crosby, *Ecological Imperialism*, p. 200.

13. In 1517 and 1518, Francisco Hernandez and Juan de Grijalva were defeated in battles against Maya along the Yucatán and Gulf coasts. Another Spaniard, Alejo García, invaded the Inca Empire from Paraguay in the early 1520s and was also driven back. In 1521, Juan Ponce de León was shot dead in Florida, and his men withdrew. The greatest native victory was the Noche Triste, or Sad Night, at Mexico City. Of about 1,200 Spaniards (the largest European force in the initial conquest wars), nearly 900 were killed. Bernal Díaz, who was there, says 860, including some deaths at Otumba. Of the sixty-nine horses present, the Aztecs killed or captured forty-six. Cortés retreated and was reinforced from Cuba, but he did not attack again until smallpox broke out in the Mexican capital a few months later. See Ronald Wright, *Stolen Continents*, p. 43.

14. If memory serves, Jimmy Carter halted the scheme after public outcry.

15. The conquest of Mexico was a two-year struggle that the Aztecs were winning until smallpox broke out. In

Peru, the hard fighting began after the judicial murder of Atahuallpa, when that Inca's half-brother Manco
besieged Cusco (the capital) and tried to burn the Spaniards out. Manco and his sons later set up an Inca free
state from which they waged guerrilla war for nearly
forty years. Modern civil wars in Peru and Guatemala
during the 1980s, in Chiapas during the 1990s, and the
1990 Oka crisis in Canada were all fuelled by unfinished
business between whites and Amerindians. However,
leaders of the Shining Path uprising in Peru were exploiters
of Peruvian nativism, not its champions.

16. Fray Motolinía, quoted in Crosby, *Columbian Exchange*,
    p. 52.

17. Francis Jennings, *The Invasion of America: Indians, Colonial-
    ism, and the Cant of Conquest* (New York: Norton, 1976),
    p. 30. This is especially true of North America and parts
    of the lowland tropics, where a century or more went by
    between the collapse of the old population and the arrival
    of the new. Like the Maya jungles, much of eastern North
    America's "virgin forest" was secondary growth on aban-
    doned Indian cornfields, towns, and park-like hunting
    lands. Jennings (essential reading, in my view) adds that
    North America was no virgin; she was a widow.

18. By 1600, the populations of Peru and Mexico had fallen
    to about a million each, losses of some 95 per cent; they
    started to recover slightly in the eighteenth century. It has
    been estimated that over the three centuries of mining at
    Potosí (Bolivia), more than a million Andean Indians died
    at the work. They were conscripted under a perversion of
    the old Inca labour tax, without any of its benefits.

19. The gold from Cajamarca weighed about seven tons;
    another three tons was stripped from Cusco. Cortés took

about a ton from Moctezuma. The true worth of the metal in contemporary Europe was far greater than its weight suggests today.

20. From *La Misère de la philosophie* ("Poverty of Philosophy"), excerpted in T. B. Bottomore and Maximilien Rubel, eds., *Karl Marx: Selected Writings in Sociology and Social Philosophy* (Harmondsworth: Pelican, 1961), p. 138.

21. In 1991, the Smithsonian put on an important exhibition called "Seeds of Change." See Viola and Margolis, *Seeds of Change*, the accompanying book, which includes articles by Alfred Crosby, William H. McNeill, and others. The potato had the added advantages that it grew well in cold climates and was hard to seize or destroy in wartime. In northern Europe, the potato gave four times the calories per acre of rye. See William H. McNeill, "American Food Crops in the Old World," in ibid., p. 45. McNeill forgets to mention that manioc (cassava), very important in West Africa, was introduced from the Americas before 1600. The American sweet potato spread throughout Southeast Asia, including China, and the Pacific. Maize has some drawbacks: it needs more water than wheat and does not give a balanced diet unless combined with beans. Nevertheless, by the late twentieth century, the tonnage of maize and potatoes produced worldwide was close to that of wheat and rice (ibid., pp. 43–44).

22. Europe had had too many people and many famines throughout much of the Middle Ages (except for a few generations of reduced land-hunger after the Black Death), but most people were still tied to the land. The potato was particularly important for population growth and industrialization in Germany and Russia.

23. In the early years of Spanish and English colonial slavery,

before the African trade took hold, native Amerindians were taken *from* America to Europe. But so many of them died that the business was not worthwhile.

24. This is also well explained for the general reader in Viola and Margolis, *Seeds of Change*.

25. Guano was dried seabird droppings that had built up to great depths on desert islands off the coast. (The word "guano" is from the Quechua *wanu*, meaning dung or manure.) In the nineteenth century, the deposits were rapidly mined out, mainly by British interests; the miners were convicts and slaves, including hundreds kidnapped from Easter Island (see notes to chapter 3). In the early twentieth century, similar deposits were found in Micronesia, on Banaba and Nauru; these are now exhausted, and there are probably no others. The common Haber-Bosch process for making chemical fertilizer combines nitrogen from the air with hydrogen from natural gas or oil.

26. See Manning, "The Oil We Eat," for an alarming analysis of the hidden costs of modern agriculture. In pre-industrial civilizations, 80 to 90 per cent of people were farmers. In North America today, only 2 per cent work the land. However, if all the people employed in farming-related machinery, petroleum, petrochemical, and freight industries are included, the true number in food production is much higher. Tim Appenzeller, "The End of Cheap Oil," *National Geographic*, June 2004, pp. 80–109, gives a good overview of the fossil-energy predicament.

27. McNeill, "American Food Crops," p. 59.

28. The Classical world had developed several kinds of machinery, including mine pumps; Hero of Alexandria invented a rudimentary steam turbine in Ptolemaic times,

but if a working model was ever made, it remained nothing more than a curiosity, like the wheeled toys of Mesoamerica or the inventions of Leonardo da Vinci. China was making cast iron from coal blast furnaces in the first millennium B.C. And Europe's Middle Ages were also more inventive than generally recognized. None of this technology "took off" anywhere until after 1492.

29. His bestselling *Royal Commentaries of the Incas* came out in 1609 in Spanish and 1688 in English, and went into several other tongues. His mother was a niece of Emperor Huayna Capac, father of Atahuallpa. Inca Garcilaso died in 1616, the same year as Shakespeare and Cervantes.

30. For Adair's quote and more on the Cherokees and Iroquois, see Wright, *Stolen Continents*, chaps. 4 and 5. A century after Franklin, Friedrich Engels was equally impressed by the Iroquois, noting among other things the balance of power between the sexes (ibid., p. 117).

31. Thirty-metre.

32. Societies of this type were seen by the Spaniards under Hernando de Soto throughout the Southeast, and the French found equally developed hierarchies along the Mississippi. Impressive earthen pyramids can still be seen at Cahokia, near modern St. Louis; at Etowah, near Atlanta; and at several other eastern sites.

33. European nations, including Britain, became more democratic than at any time since their humble beginnings a thousand years before. At home, that is; democracy was not for the empires.

34. See Fukuyama, *End of History*.

35. Published in 1898. Wells wrote the story as a satire, with the great colonizers (the British at the height of their empire) suddenly finding themselves outclassed by spacefaring

conquerors. He decided to give it a happy ending: in this
case, disease works against, not for, the invaders.

36. The serpent persuades Eve to eat from the Tree of Knowledge (or Life) so that "your eyes shall be opened, and ye
shall be as gods."

37. The Popol Vuh text, written in Quiché using the Roman
alphabet, comes from sixteenth-century highland Guatemala but includes mythology dating from the Classic
Period. Parts of it may have been transcribed from pre-
Columbian glyphic texts. It is tempting to think that the
cautionary "Rebellion of the Tools" parable is an echo of
the Classic fall in the ninth century.

38. Delia Goetz, Sylvanus Morley, and Adrián Recinos, trans.,
Popol Vuh: The Sacred Book of the Ancient Quiché Maya
(Norman: University of Oklahoma, 1950), pp. 91–92. For
another good translation, see Dennis Tedlock, *Popol Vuh*
(New York: Simon and Schuster, 1985).

39. From Dickens's portrait of "Coketown" in *Hard Times*
([1854] 1969, p. 65): "It was a town of machinery and
tall chimneys, out of which interminable serpents of
smoke trailed themselves for ever and ever, and never
got uncoiled. It had a black canal in it, and a river that
ran purple with ill-smelling dye, and vast piles of building full of windows where there was a rattling and a
trembling all day long, and where the piston of the
steam-engine worked monotonously up and down, like
the head of an elephant in a state of melancholy madness. It contained several large streets all very like one
another, and small streets still more like one another,
inhabited by people equally like one another, who all
went in and out at the same hours, with the same sound
upon the same pavements, to do the same work, and to

whom every day was the same as yesterday and tomorrow."

40. From *Coningsby*, published in 1844.

41. Yearly spending on weapons by Europe's Great Powers was £158 million in 1890, £288 million in 1910, and £397 million in 1914 (see Eric Hobsbawm, *The Age of Empire, 1875–1914* [New York: Random House, 1987], p. 350). Ibsen's *An Enemy of the People*, an 1882 play about polluted water and corrupt civic practices, is one of the first environmentalist works. See Ibsen [1882] 1979.

42. Some estimates for the Great War are in the 15 to 20 million range. The great influenza pandemic, which may have incubated in the trenches and field hospitals, killed a further 20 to 40 million worldwide.

43. Estimates for the dead of the two world wars, including victims of famine, massacre, and persecution, run as high as 187 million. See Martin Rees, *Our Final Century: Will the Human Race Survive the Twenty-first Century?* (London: Heinemann, 2003), p. 25. The book is published in North America as *Our Final Hour*.

44. Mad cow is technically bovine spongiform encephalopathy, or BSE. In humans it is usually called Creutzfeldt-Jakob disease, or CJD. It is now clear that humans can catch the bovine form from eating tainted meat, especially if it contains any brain or spinal-cord tissue, which was often used as a binder in hamburgers and meat pies. This complex of diseases, which includes scrapie in sheep and *kuru* in New Guineans who practise ritual cannibalism, is neither viral nor bacterial and cannot be destroyed by normal sterilization procedures. Still not fully understood, it is thought to be caused by a self-replicating protein named a prion. The incubation period

in humans is thought to be long, from several years to as
many as thirty.

45. Wright, *A Scientific Romance*, chap. 4.

46. Four-and-a-half-metre.

47. From an Agence France Press report carried in the *Globe
and Mail* on March 24, 2004.

48. Margaret Atwood, *Oryx and Crake* (Toronto: McClelland
and Stewart, 2003), chap. 6.

49. Americans seem to elect such people at least once a generation (though they can't exactly be blamed for *electing*
George W. Bush in 2000). Like Bush with the Kyoto
Accord, Reagan refused to sign the international Law of
the Sea Treaty, thus condemning the world to decades
more of unsafe tankers, toxic dumping, overfishing, and
the exploitation of seamen on ships registered under flags
of convenience, such as Liberia.

50. Much of the worst environmental destruction by both systems since 1945 was caused by the arms race of the Cold
War. Without that, both might have been easier on their
surroundings (and kinder to the people under their control). Engels's view that "the productivity of the land can
be infinitely increased by the application of capital, labour
and science" (quoted in Ponting, *Green History*, p. 158)
might easily have been uttered by an arch capitalist. Such
nineteenth-century optimism, born in a time when the natural world was still vast and human impact less than a fiftieth
of what it is now, lies at the root of our present impasse.

51. Pesticide contamination in Rocky Mountain lakes has
been found to be greater than on the prairies where the
chemicals are sprayed. The same is true of the poles. Con-
taminants pervade the atmosphere and condense in cold,
"pristine" places.

52. Tainter, *Complex Societies*, p. 214. Tainter is an archaeologist. One might object that his eyes are fixed too firmly on the rear-view mirror. This is what the cheerleaders of progress will say, for a belief in modern exceptionalism — that the old rules don't apply to us — is the keystone of their disbelief in limits. But a growing number of "hard" scientists has begun to share the archaeologists', ecologists', and satirists' concerns.

53. According to the press, this report was commissioned by the long-time Pentagon adviser Andrew Marshall (*Globe and Mail*, February 24, 2004, referring to stories in the *Observer* and in *Fortune* magazine). Since Rio, the 1990s have overtaken the 1980s as the warmest decade on record, and the European summer of 2003 was the hottest ever recorded.

54. Rees, *Our Final Century*, pp. 8, 24. He adds: "Our choices and actions could ensure the perpetual future of life. . . . Or in contrast, through malign intent, or through misadventure, twenty-first-century technology could jeopardise life's potential." Rees is especially worried by potential rogue technologies, such as bioengineering, nanotechnology, cybernetics, and certain "doomsday" experiments on the frontiers of physics. As an astronomer, he advocates establishing a small human colony in space as soon as possible, to give intelligent life a second chance if things go wrong. But if we ruin the earth, are we intelligent? And why should we deserve another chance?

55. Declassification of American and Soviet sources from the 1962 Cuban Missile Crisis, and statements by those involved, show that the world came much closer to nuclear war than had been thought. Robert McNamara, then U.S. defence secretary, has written "we came within a hairbreadth without realising it." See ibid., pp. 25–28.

56. Following controversial legal rulings in the United States, biotech and agribusiness companies have taken out patents on crops (and even animals) they claim to have "invented." In fact, not even *one* new food staple has been developed from a wild plant since prehistoric times. All of our crop science — whether selective breeding or genetic manipulation — is mere piggybacking on the work of ancient civilizations. Appropriate research should be rewarded, but if we are going to allow private property rights over ancient food staples, then royalties should be paid to the heirs of the true inventors, most of whom are struggling peasants who need the cash a lot more than Monsanto. Small wonder the have-not countries are suspicious of the rich countries' motives in aggressively promoting hybrid and engineered staples that threaten to contaminate and destroy the crop diversity that still exists in agriculture's old heartlands.

57. American Secretary of State Colin Powell has said that AIDS is a far greater threat than terrorism.

58. Because of the mother's iodine deficiency during pregnancy. (These figures come from the Micronutrient Initiative, Ottawa, and were reported in "'Hidden Hunger' Weakens Physical, Economic Health," André Picard, *Globe and Mail*, March 25, 2004.) The statistics on water deaths come from Ponting, *Green History*, p. 351.

59. Reckoning those killed in the two world wars and the Russian Revolution.

60. Many of these policies were developed by the Bretton Woods Agreements of 1944, under the influence of John Maynard Keynes. Earlier forms of social safety net were already in place, notably Franklin Roosevelt's New Deal. The postwar era, from the 1950s to the 1970s, has been

dubbed the "Golden Age" by the historian Eric Hobsbawm in his magisterial survey of the twentieth century, *The Age of Extremes: A History of the World 1914–1991* (London: Michael Joseph, 1994). Margaret MacMillan points out that the speedy postwar implementation of the Marshall Plan was stimulated by the threat of "a single, clear enemy . . . the Soviet Union" (MacMillan, *Paris 1919: Six Months That Changed the World* [New York: Random House, 2001], p. 61).

61. John Kenneth Galbraith, speaking at the Harvard Club, Toronto, 1994.

62. Especially since the 1929 Wall Street crash. One of the best descriptions of what conditions were like in the subsequent Great Slump is to be found in James Agee and Walker Evans's *Let Us Now Praise Famous Men* (New York: Ballantine, 1966). The conditions of the Dirty Thirties (the American dust bowl) are often blamed on drought, but their severity and the huge losses to erosion were caused mainly by bad farming practices in unsuitable environments. The dry plains are best left to the buffalo, who could probably provide us with as much food as we get from farming if wild or semi-wild herds were efficiently managed. See, for example, Manning, "Oil We Eat."

63. Between 1950 and the late 1970s, beggars and homeless people were nearly unknown in the First World. The practical consequence of deregulation has been a return to social Darwinism — a late-Victorian perversion of evolutionary thought that claims the poor are poor because they're inferior, and the best thing for the progress of the human race is to let them die on the street.

64. In 1900, the world still had untouched forests and fisheries, untapped oil reserves, unused hydroelectric potential,

and vast expanses of farmland in prime condition. The amount of farmland per person has declined by 20 per cent in the past ten years. Production is maintained by industrial techniques that treat earth as little more than a hydroponic medium for chemicals. Groundwater is becoming contaminated and exhausted. In his book, published in 1991, Clive Ponting singled out Rwanda as an example of the gulf between the First and Third worlds, noting that the average Rwandan's income was one-hundredth of the average American's. Three years later, nearly a million Rwandans died in the worst genocide since the Second World War. Reckoning the dead as a proportion of population, this was the equivalent of slaughtering 35 million in the United States. The twenty-first century may have begun in Rwanda, not New York.

65. United Nations Human Development Report, released September 9, 1998. For a summary of highlights, see the *Daily Telegraph*, September 10, 1998. The three were Bill Gates (Microsoft), Helen Walton (Wal-Mart), and Warren Buffett (investor), with US$51 billion, $48 billion, and $33 billion, respectively. The report estimates that a child born in the United States, Britain, or France will, in its lifetime, consume and pollute more than fifty children do in the poor nations. It also estimates that in 1998, only $40 billion was needed to bring basic health, education, clean water, and sanitation to the world's poorest citizens. Gates alone could afford that and still have $11 billion left; he also owns more than the poorest 100 million Americans combined. Other sources indicate that within the United States, the ratio between the salary of a CEO and that of a shop-floor worker has soared from 39:1 in the late 1970s to about 1,000:1 today. See John Ralston Saul, "The Collapse

of Globalism," *Harper's*, March 2004, p. 38, and *The Unconscious Civilization* (Toronto: Anansi, 1995), p. 14.

66. United Nations Human Development Report.

67. Sometimes "good" environmental policy can backfire. Brazilian scientists have reported that 9,300 square miles (24,000 square kilometres) of Amazon rainforest were lost in 2003 alone. Much of this was caused by the clearing of new land on which to raise beef and soybeans for the booming (mainly European) demand in GM-free food (BBC World News, April 8, 2004).

68. A state of affairs maintained, to a large degree, by the consumerist pornography of advertising.

69. George W. Bush's astronomical deficits seem designed to cripple the American state in all fields except the military. The result, if this goes on, will be to make America more like Latin America, where the army is often the only effective public institution.

70. James Watt, speaking in 1981. As noted above, social Darwinism claims that the poor are inferior, and that the best thing for the progress of the human race is to let them die.

71. Bush's attorney general, John Ashcroft, has said, "In America, there is no king but Jesus." See Lewis Lapham, "Reading the Mail," *Harper's*, November 2003, p. 9.

72. Crosby, *Ecological Imperialism*, p. 92. See Laurie Garrett, *The Coming Plague: Newly Emerging Diseases in a World Out of Balance* (New York: Penguin, 1994), for a survey of potential medical catastrophes.

BIBLIOGRAPHY

Adams, Robert McCormick. *The Evolution of Urban Society: Early Mesopotamia and Prehispanic Mexico.* London: Weidenfeld and Nicholson, 1966.

———. *Heartland of Cities: Surveys of Ancient Settlement and Land Use on the Central Floodplain of the Euphrates.* Chicago: University of Chicago Press, 1981.

Agee, James, and Walker Evans. *Let Us Now Praise Famous Men.* New York: Ballantine, 1966. First published in 1939.

Allchin, Bridget, and Raymond Allchin. *The Birth of Indian Civilization.* Harmondsworth, UK: Pelican, 1968.

Alley, Richard. *The Two-Mile Time Machine: Ice Cores, Abrupt Climate Change, and Our Future.* Princeton, NJ: Princeton University Press, 2000.

Appenzeller, Tim. "The End of Cheap Oil." *National Geographic,* June 2004, 80–109.

Arens, W. *The Man-Eating Myth: Anthropology and Anthropophagy.* New York: Oxford University Press, 1979.

Atwood, Margaret. *The Handmaid's Tale.* Toronto: McClelland and Stewart, 1985.

————. *Oryx and Crake*. Toronto: McClelland and Stewart, 2003.

Bahn, Paul, and John Flenley. *Easter Island, Earth Island*. London: Thames and Hudson, 1992.

Bolin, Inge. "Our Apus Are Dying!: Glacial Retreat and Its Consequences for Life in the Andes." Paper presented at the American Anthropological Association meetings, Chicago, Illinois, November 19, 2003.

Bottomore, T. B., and Maximilien Rubel, eds. *Karl Marx: Selected Writings in Sociology and Social Philosophy*. Harmondsworth, UK: Pelican, 1961.

Braudel, Fernand. *The Structures of Everyday Life*. New York: Harper and Row, 1981.

————. *The Wheels of Commerce: Civilization and Capitalism 15th–18th Century*. New York: Harper and Row, 1982.

Braun, Barbara. *Pre-Columbian Art and the Post-Columbian World: Ancient American Sources of Modern Art*. New York: Abrams, 1993.

Brody, Hugh. *The Other Side of Eden: Hunters, Farmers and the Shaping of the World*. Vancouver: Douglas and McIntyre, 2000.

Brotherson, Gordon. *Book of the Fourth World: Reading the Native Americas through Their Literature*. Cambridge: Cambridge University Press, 1992.

Butler, Samuel. *Erewhon*. 1872. Reprint, Harmondsworth, UK: Penguin, 1970.

Chang Kwang-Chih. *Early Chinese Civilization: Anthropological Perspectives*. Cambridge, MA: Harvard University Press, 1976.

Childe, Gordon. *New Light on the Most Ancient East*. London: Routledge and Kegan Paul, 1954.

————. *What Happened in History*. Harmondsworth, UK: Pelican, 1964.

Chua, Amy. *World on Fire: How Exporting Free Market Democracy Breeds Ethnic Hatred and Global Instability*. New York: Anchor, 2004.

Clarke, Peter. *Hope and Glory: Britain 1900–1990*. London: Penguin, 1996.

Clendinnen, Inga. *Aztecs: An Interpretation*. Cambridge: Cambridge University Press, 1991.

———. *Reading the Holocaust*. Melbourne: Text, 1998.

Coe, Michael D. *The Maya*. London: Thames and Hudson, 1987.

———. *Breaking the Maya Code*. London: Thames and Hudson, 1992.

Coetzee, J. M. *Waiting for the Barbarians*. London: Penguin, 1982.

Cohen, Mark Nathan. *The Food Crisis in Prehistory: Overpopulation and the Origins of Agriculture*. New Haven, CN: Yale University Press, 1977.

Conrad, Geoffrey W., and Arthur A. Demarest. *Religion and Empire*. Cambridge: Cambridge University Press, 1984.

Conrad, Joseph. *The Secret Agent*. Harmondsworth, UK: Penguin, 1936. Originally published in 1907.

Crosby, Alfred. *The Columbian Exchange: Biological and Cultural Consequences of 1492*. Westport, CN: Greenwood Press, 1972.

———. *Ecological Imperialism: The Biological Expansion of Europe 900–1900*. Cambridge: Cambridge University Press, 1986.

Culbert, T. Patrick, and Don S. Rice, eds. *Precolumbian Population History in the Maya Lowlands*. Albuquerque: University of New Mexico Press, 1990.

Daniel, Glyn. *The Idea of Prehistory*. Harmondsworth, UK: Pelican, 1962.

Davis, Wade. *One River: Explorations and Discoveries in the Amazon Rain Forest*. New York: Simon & Schuster, 1996.

Daws, Gavan. *A Dream of Islands*. Honolulu: Mutual Publishing, 1980.

Denevan, William. "The Pristine Myth: The Landscape of the Americas in 1492." In *The Americas Before and After Columbus*. Edited by Karl Butzer. Oxford: Blackwell, 1992.

Diamond, Jared. *Guns, Germs, and Steel: The Fates of Human Societies*. New York: W. W. Norton, 1997.

Dickens, Charles. *Hard Times*. Harmondsworth, UK: Penguin, 1969. Originally published in 1854.

Dillehay, Tom D., ed. *Monte Verde: A Late Pleistocene Settlement in Chile*. Washington, DC: Smithsonian Books, 1989.

Edwards, Clinton R. "Possibilities of Pre-Columbian Maritime Contacts among New World Civilizations." In *Pre-Columbian Contact within Nuclear America*. Edited by J. C. Kelley and C. L. Riley. Carbondale: University Southern Illinois University Press, 1969.

Eiseley, Loren. *The Invisible Pyramid*. New York: Scribner's, 1970.

———. *The Star Thrower*. New York: Harcourt Brace Jovanovich, 1978.

Fisher, W. B. *The Middle East: A Physical, Social and Regional Geography*. London: Methuen, 1978.

Flannery, Tim. *The Future Eaters: An Ecological History of the Australasian Lands and People*. New York: Braziller, 1995.

Fowler, Melvin. "A Pre-Columbian Urban Center on the Mississippi." *Scientific American* 23, no. 2 (August 1975): 92–101.

Frye, Northrop. "Humanities in a New World." In *Three Lectures* by Northrop Frye, Clyde Kluckhohn, and V. B. Wigglesworth. Toronto: University of Toronto Press, 1958.

Fukuyama, Francis. *The End of History and the Last Man*. New York: Free Press, 1992.

Galeano, Eduardo. "Did History Lie When It Promised Peace and Progress?" In *Guatemala in Rebellion: Unfinished History.* Edited by Jonathan Fried et al. New York: Grove, 1983.

Garrett, Laurie. *The Coming Plague: Newly Emerging Diseases in a World Out of Balance.* New York: Penguin, 1994.

Gibbon, Edward. *The History of the Decline and Fall of the Roman Empire.* London: Folio Society, 1995. Originally published in 1776.

Goetz, Delia, Sylvanus Morley, and Adrián Recinos, trans. *Popol Vuh: The Sacred Book of the Ancient Quiché Maya.* Norman: University of Oklahoma, 1950.

Golding, William. *The Inheritors.* London: Faber and Faber, 1955.

―――. *Pincher Martin.* London: Faber and Faber, 1956.

Gorst, Martin. *Measuring Eternity: The Search for the Beginning of Time.* New York: Broadway Books, 2001.

Goudie, Andrew. *The Human Impact on the Natural Environment.* Oxford: Blackwell, 2000.

Grady, Wayne. *The Quiet Limit of the World: A Journey to the North Pole to Investigate Global Warming.* Toronto: Macfarlane Walter and Ross, 1997.

Harlan, Jack R. *Crops and Man.* Madison, WI: American Society of Agronomy: Crop Science Society of America, 1992.

Harth, Erich. *Dawn of a Millennium: Beyond Evolution and Culture.* London: Penguin, 1990.

Heintzman, Andrew, and Evan Solomon, eds. *Fueling the Future: How the Battle Over Energy Is Changing Everything.* Toronto: Anansi, 2003.

Hemming, John. *The Conquest of the Incas.* Harmondsworth, UK: Penguin, 1983.

Henry, Donald, et al. "Human Behavioral Organization in the Middle Paleolithic: Were Neanderthals Different?" *American Anthropologist* 106, no. 1 (March 2004): 17–31.

Heyerdahl, Thor. "Guara Navigation: Indigenous Sailing off the Andean Coast." *Southwestern Journal of Anthropology* 13, no. 2 (1957).

———. *Sea Routes to Polynesia*. London: Allen and Unwin, 1968.

Heyerdahl, Thor, and Arne Skjolsvold. "Archaeological Evidence of Pre-Spanish Visits to the Galápagos Islands." *Memoirs of the Society for American Archaeology*, no. 12 (1956).

Hoban, Russell. *Riddley Walker*. London: Jonathan Cape, 1980.

Hobsbawm, Eric. *The Age of Empire, 1875–1914*. New York: Random House, 1987.

———. *The Age of Extremes: A History of the World 1914–1991*. London: Michael Joseph, 1994.

Homer-Dixon, Thomas. *The Ingenuity Gap: How Can We Solve the Problems of the Future?* Toronto: Knopf, 2000.

Hosler, Dorothy. "Ancient West Mexican Metallurgy: South and Central American Origins and West Mexican Transformations." *American Anthropologist* 90, no. 4 (1988): 832–55.

Howells, William. *Mankind in the Making: The Story of Human Evolution*. London: Secker and Warburg, 1960.

Huxley, Aldous. *Brave New World*. London: Chatto and Windus, 1932.

———. *Beyond the Mexique Bay*. London: Paladin, 1984. Originally published in 1934.

Ibsen, Henrik. *An Enemy of the People*. Translated by Arthur Miller. New York: Penguin Books, 1979. Originally published in 1882.

Jacobs, Jane. *The Economy of Cities*. New York: Random House, 1969.

———. *Dark Age Ahead*. Toronto: Random House, 2004.

Jay, Nancy. *Throughout Your Generations Forever: Sacrifice,*

Religion, and Paternity. Chicago: University of Chicago Press, 1992.

Jennings, Francis. *The Invasion of America: Indians, Colonialism, and the Cant of Conquest.* New York: W. W. Norton, 1976.

Kelley, David H. *Deciphering the Maya Script.* Austin: University of Texas, 1976.

Kolata, Alan. *Tiwanaku and Its Hinterland: Archaeology and Paleoecology of an Andean Civilization.* Washington, DC: Smithsonian Books, 1996.

Lanning, Edward. *Peru before the Incas.* Englewood Cliffs, NJ: Prentice-Hall, 1967.

Lapham, Lewis. "Reading the Mail." *Harper's,* November 2003, 9–11.

Leakey, Richard, and Roger Lewin. *Origins Reconsidered: In Search of What Makes Us Human.* New York: Doubleday, 1992.

Lee, Richard. *The Dobe !Kung.* New York: Holt Rinehart and Winston, 1984.

Leslie, John. *The End of the World: The Science and Ethics of Human Extinction.* London: Routledge, 1998.

Limerick, Patricia Nelson. *Something in the Soil: Legacies and Reckonings in the New West.* New York: W. W. Norton, 2000.

Lindqvist, Sven. *Exterminate All the Brutes.* Translated by Joan Tate. London: Granta Books, 1996.

Livingston, John A. *Rogue Primate: An Exploration of Human Domestication.* Toronto: Key Porter, 1994.

Lovell, W. George. *Conquest and Survival in Colonial Guatemala: A Historical Geography of the Cuchumatán Highlands 1500–1821,* 2nd ed. Montreal: McGill-Queen's University Press, 1992.

———. *A Beauty That Hurts: Life and Death in Guatemala.* Austin: University of Texas Press, 2000.

Lovell, W. George, and Christopher H. Lutz. *Demography and*

Empire: A Guide to the Population History of Spanish Central America, 1500–1821. Boulder, CO: Westview, 1995.

Lovell, W. George, and David Cook Noble, eds. *Secret Judgments of God: Old World Disease in Colonial Spanish America*. Norman: University of Oklahoma Press, 1992.

Lynas, Mark. *High Tide: News from a Warming World*. London: Flamingo, 2004.

MacMillan, Margaret. *Paris 1919: Six Months That Changed the World*. New York: Random House, 2001.

Mallowan, M. E. L. *Early Mesopotamia and Iran*. London: Thames and Hudson, 1965.

Malthus, Thomas. *An Essay on the Principle of Population*. Edited by Anthony Flew. London: Penguin, 1970. Originally published in 1798 and 1830 (revised).

Mann, Charles. "1491." *Atlantic Monthly*, March 2002, 41–53.

Manning, Richard. "The Oil We Eat." *Harper's*, February 2004, 37–45.

Martin, Paul S. "Prehistoric Overkill: The Global Model." In *Quaternary Extinctions: A Prehistoric Revolution*. Edited by Paul S. Martin and Richard G. Klein. Tucson: University of Arizona Press, 1984.

Marx, Karl. *Karl Marx: Selected Writings in Sociology and Social Philosophy*. Edited by T. B. Bottomore and Maximilien Rubel. Harmondsworth, UK: Pelican, 1961.

McKibben, Bill. *The End of Nature*. New York: Random House, 1989.

McNeill, William H. *Plagues and Peoples*. New York: Anchor, 1976.

Mellaart, James. *Earliest Civilizations of the Near East*. London: Thames and Hudson, 1965.

———. *Çatal Hüyük: A Neolithic Town in Anatolia*. London: Thames and Hudson, 1967.

Menchú, Rigoberta. *I, Rigoberta Menchú: An Indian Woman*

in Guatemala. Translated by Ann Wright. London: Verso, 1984.

Millones, Luis. "The Time of the Inca: The Colonial Indians' Quest." *Antiquity* no. 66 (1992): 204–16.

Mitchell, Alanna. *Dancing at the Dead Sea: Tracking the World's Environmental Hotspots*. Toronto: Key Porter, 2004.

Mitchell, Timothy. "The Object of Development: America's Egypt." In Jonathan Crush, ed., *The Power of Development*. London: Routledge, 1995.

Mittelstaedt, Martin. "Some Like It Hot." *Globe and Mail*, April 17, 2004.

———. "The Larder Is Almost Bare." *Globe and Mail*, May 22, 2004.

Moseley, Michael E. *The Incas and Their Ancestors: The Archaeology of Peru*. London: Thames and Hudson, 1992.

Mowat, Farley. *Sea of Slaughter*. Toronto: McClelland and Stewart, 1984.

National Research Council. *Lost Crops of the Incas*. Washington, DC: National Academy Press, 1989.

Newhouse, John. *Imperial America: The Bush Assault on the World Order*. New York: Knopf, 2003.

Nikiforuk, Andrew. *The Fourth Horseman: A Short History of Epidemics, Plagues, Famine, and Other Scourges*. Toronto: Viking, 1991.

Oppenheim, A. Leo. *Ancient Mesopotamia: Portrait of a Dead Civilization*. Rev. ed. Chicago: University of Chicago Press, 1977.

Orliac, Catherine, and Michel Orliac. *Easter Island: Mystery of the Stone Giants*. Translated by Paul G. Bahn. New York: Abrams, 1995.

Orwell, George. *Nineteen Eighty-four*. London: Secker and Warburg, 1949.

Ovid (Publius Ovidius Naso). *Amores*. Translated by Guy Lee.

London: John Murray, 1968. Republished in 2000 as *Ovid in Love*.

Pardo, Luis A., ed. *Saqsaywaman* no. 1 (July 1970): 144.

Pizarro, Pedro. *Relación del Descubrimiento y Conquista de los Reinos del Perú*. Edited by Guillermo Lohmann Villena. Lima: Universidad Católica, 1986. Originally written in 1571.

Pollard, Sidney. *The Idea of Progress: History and Society*. London: C. A. Watts, 1968.

Ponting, Clive. *A Green History of the World: The Environment and the Collapse of Great Civilizations*. London: Sinclair-Stevenson, 1991.

Redman, Charles. *Human Impact on Ancient Environments*. Tucson: University of Arizona Press, 1999.

Rees, Martin. *Our Final Century*. London: William Heinemann / Random House, 2003. Published in North America as *Our Final Hour*.

Roggeveen, Jacob. *The Journal of Jacob Roggeveen*. Translated and edited by Andrew Sharp. Oxford: Clarendon Press, 1970.

Routledge, Katherine S. *The Mystery of Easter Island*. London: Sifton, Praed and Co., 1919.

Safdie, Moshe. *The City After the Automobile: An Architect's Vision*. Toronto: Stoddart, 1997.

Safina, Carl. *Song for the Blue Ocean: Encounters Along the World's Coasts and Beneath the Seas*. New York: Henry Holt / John Macrae, 1997.

Sahlins, Marshall David. *Stone Age Economics*. London: Tavistock Publications, 1972.

Sandars, N. K., trans. *The Epic of Gilgamesh*. Harmondsworth, UK: Penguin, 1972.

Saul, John Ralston. *The Unconscious Civilization*. Toronto: Anansi, 1995.

———. "The Collapse of Globalism." *Harper's*, March 2004, 33–43.

Scarre, Chris. *Past Worlds: The Times Atlas of Archaeology*. London: Times Books, 1988.

Schele, Linda, and David Freidel. *A Forest of Kings: The Untold Story of the Ancient Maya*. New York: Morrow, 1990.

Schumacher, E. F. *Small Is Beautiful: A Study of Economics As If People Mattered*. London: Abacus, 1973.

Sharer, Robert J. *The Ancient Maya*. Stanford, CA: Stanford University Press, 1994.

Stanish, Charles. *Ancient Titicaca: The Evolution of Complex Society in Southern Peru and Northern Bolivia*. Princeton, NJ: Princeton University Press, 2004.

Steadman, David. "Prehistoric Extinctions of Pacific Island Birds." *Science* no. 267 (February 1995): 1123–31.

Stringer, Christopher, and Robin McKie. *African Exodus: The Origins of Modern Humanity*. New York: Henry Holt/John Macrae, 1997.

Tainter, Joseph A. *The Collapse of Complex Societies*. Cambridge: Cambridge University Press, 1988.

Tattersall, Ian. *The Last Neanderthal: The Rise, Success, and Mysterious Extinction of Our Closest Human Relatives*. New York: Westview Press, 1999.

Tedlock, Barbara. *Time and the Highland Maya*. Albuquerque: University of New Mexico Press, 1982.

Thompson, J. Eric S. *The Rise and Fall of Maya Civilization*. London: Pimlico, 1993. Originally published in 1954.

———. *Maya Hieroglyphic Writing*. Norman: University of Oklahoma Press, 1971.

Thoreau, Henry David. *Walden: Or, Life in the Woods*. New York: New American Library/Signet, 1960. Originally published in 1854.

Trigger, Bruce. *Early Civilizations: Ancient Egypt in Context*.

Cairo: American University in Cairo Press, 1993.

Trinkaus, Erik, and Pat Shipman. *The Neanderthals: Changing the Image of Mankind*. New York: Knopf, 1993.

Tudge, Colin. *So Shall We Reap*. London: Allen Lane, 2003.

Viola, Herman, and Carolyn Margolis, eds. *Seeds of Change: A Quincentennial Commemoration*. Washington, DC: Smithsonian Institution Press, 1991.

Waldman, Carl. *Atlas of the North American Indian*. New York: Facts on File, 1985.

Watson, William. *China*. London: Thames and Hudson, 1961.

Weatherford, Jack. *Indian Givers: How the Indians of the Americas Transformed the World*. New York: Crown, 1988.

———. *Native Roots: How the Indians Enriched America*. New York: Crown, 1991.

Webster, David. *The Fall of the Ancient Maya: Solving the Mystery of the Maya Collapse*. London: Thames and Hudson, 2002.

Wells, H. G. "The Grisly Folk." *Selected Short Stories*. London: Penguin, 1958.

Wells, H. G., Julian S. Huxley, and G. P. Wells. *The Science of Life*. New York: Doubleday, 1929.

Wenke, Robert J. *Patterns in Prehistory*. Oxford: Oxford University Press, 1980.

Wheatley, Paul. *The Pivot of the Four Quarters: A Preliminary Enquiry into the Origins and Character of the Ancient Chinese City*. Edinburgh: Edinburgh University Press, 1971.

White, Lynn. "The Historical Roots of Our Ecologic Crisis." *Science* 155, no. 3767 (March 1967): 1203–1207.

Wilson, J. A. "Egypt through the New Kingdom: Civilization without Cities." In *City Invincible*. Edited by C. H. Kraeling and Robert McCormick Adams. Chicago: University of Chicago Press, 1960.

Wright, Ronald. *Time Among the Maya*. London: Bodley Head, 1989.

————. *Stolen Continents: Conquest and Resistance in the Americas.* Boston: Houghton Mifflin, 1992.

————. *A Scientific Romance.* London: Anchor, 1997.

————. "Civilization Is a Pyramid Scheme." *Globe and Mail,* August 5, 2000.

————. "All Hooked Up to Monkey Brains." *Times Literary Supplement,* May 16, 2003.

Wyndham, John. *The Day of the Triffids.* London: Michael Joseph, 1951.

————. *The Chrysalids.* London: Michael Joseph, 1955.

INDEX

The CBC Massey Lectures Series